MW01172859

MORE PRAISE FOR
THE RESILIENCE ROADMAP

Mark has created an absolute must-read for anyone facing challenges in today's world. His approach to moving through these challenges is both practical and insightful. Using his roadmap as a guide and his personal experiences and anecdotes to drive home the ever-growing importance for resilience today.

This roadmap will certainly support people in navigating any kind of challenge in any kind of season.

—Heather Moyse
Speaker, author of *Redefining 'Realistic,'*
Founder of The Possibility Playground,
and Two-Time Olympic Champion

Mark Black reminds us that human beings are fundamentally resilient, but in today's demanding world we all need to proactively strengthen it. His book, *The Resilience Roadmap*, offers just the guide. In it he shares helpful strategies, interwoven with his own remarkable story of strength and spirit. For less stress and more success, read this book.

—Michelle Cederberg, CSP
Author of *Energy Now!* and *The Success-Energy Equation*

Mark has become an expert on building resilience and courage, inspiring people to live life to its fullest. His new book takes his writing and leadership to another level and provides the reader with a clear path on how to build resilience in their life so that they can overcome challenges that they are faced with—no matter how difficult.

Although in the book Mark says, "The world needs people like you more than ever," while referring to us the readers, the reality is that we need Mark more than ever. The messages in *The Resilience Roadmap* have never been more important."

—Greg Wells Ph.D.
Author of *The Ripple Effect and Rest, Refocus, Recharge*

The best teachers are those who have achieved what they teach and helped others do the same. Mark is one of those teachers. This book lays out clear strategies for summoning resilience when life, inevitably, gets challenging.

—Josh Shipp
Founder of Top Youth Speakers®

This is a practical and meaningful book that relates to everyone. Mark's experiences and insight and heart are there to guide readers to a greater mindset for resiliency.

—Marcus Engel
Author of *"I'm Here: Compassionate Communication in Patient Care"*
and host of the Compassion & Courage podcast

I had the extreme pleasure of knowing Mark as a student in my grade five Math class and also the shared experience of being with him at the hospital as he desperately waited for a heart and lung transplant. Living his life to the fullest and acknowledging the resilience needed just to live a normal life has been Mark's mission. He is a role model and a great reminder of how we should live our lives.

As Mark states, change is not going away and resilience is complex. For a workplace requiring all of your patience and energy just to go to work every day or for daily family and personal experiences, Mark provides strategies and support as you navigate your everyday world. Thank you, Mark, for writing so we can all learn from you.

Be selfish and read this book.

—Karen Power
Co-Author of *Leading with Intention*

THE
RESILIENCE
ROADMAP

7 Guideposts for

Charting Your Course

in a Chaotic World

THE RESILIENCE ROADMAP

7 Guideposts for Charting Your Course in a Chaotic World

MARK BLACK

PYP **Publish** Your Purpose

For permission requests, write to the publisher, addressed "Attention: Permissions Coordinator," at the address below.

Publish Your Purpose
141 Weston Street, #155
Hartford, CT, 06141

The opinions expressed by the Author are not necessarily those held by Publish Your Purpose.

Ordering Information: Quantity sales and special discounts are available on quantity purchases by corporations, associations, and others. For details, contact the publisher at hello@publishyourpurpose.com.

Edited by: Nancy Graham-Tillman
Cover design by: Cornelia Murariu
Typeset by: Medlar Publishing Solutions Pvt Ltd., India

Printed in the United States of America.

ISBN: 979-8-88797-022-6 (hardcover)
ISBN: 979-8-88797-021-9 (paperback)
ISBN: 979-8-88797-023-3 (ebook)

Library of Congress Control Number: 2022923587

First edition, June 2023.

The information contained within this book is strictly for informational purposes. The material may include information, products, or services by third parties. As such, the Author and Publisher do not assume responsibility or liability for any third-party material or opinions. The publisher is not responsible for websites (or their content) that are not owned by the publisher. Readers are advised to do their own due diligence when it comes to making decisions.

Publish Your Purpose is a hybrid publisher of nonfiction books. Our mission is to elevate the voices often excluded from traditional publishing. We intentionally seek out authors and storytellers with diverse backgrounds, life experiences, and unique perspectives to publish books that will make an impact in the world. Do you have a book idea you would like us to consider publishing? Please visit PublishYourPurpose.com for more information.

For
Marise, Emma, Matteo, and Caleb,
you are my world.
I love you.

&

For
my donor and their family.
This would not have been possible
without your selfless gift.
Thank you.

CONTENTS

INTRODUCTION

Sitting at the gate waiting to board our plane, we watched the large television screen showing one of the twenty-four hour news channels. The typical red banner headlines didn't immediately grab my attention; they have become such a common tool used by these channels to keep us glued to their broadcasts that I've learned to tune them out for the most part. What caught my attention was how many people around me were also tuning in. There was already a sense that something significant was happening.

I watched for a few minutes as a broadcaster reported that the virus in China we'd been hearing about had now infected several dozen passengers on a cruise ship in California. The virus, it seemed, was spreading farther and faster than it had thus far, and speculation was beginning about whether the World Health Organization would soon officially declare this a global pandemic.

Even as someone with a compromised immune system, I wasn't particularly alarmed. I was travelling with my whole family (wife, kids, brothers and their families, and my parents). We were on our way back from a week in the sun in Florida. Because of my weakened immune system, I opted to wear a mask on the flight as a precautionary measure, but I was in the minority. While the report was somewhat concerning, everyone went about their business as normal. If you had turned away from the monitor and looked around the airport terminal and everyone in it, you would've had no idea the world was about to change dramatically.

By the following morning, our local provincial government was beginning to take action. This was the end of spring break for tens of thousands of students and teachers and the start of the break for thousands more. Our local government announced that anyone still in the US would be subject to a two-week quarantine when they arrived. Today that word has become so commonplace it hardly registers, but at that stage of the pandemic, the idea that people would have to stay at home and not be allowed to go out was groundbreaking. We were beginning to understand how serious the situation was and how dramatically it would affect every aspect of our lives.

For me, the first thing that was impacted was my business. I'm a professional keynote speaker. At that time, ninety-five percent of my annual income came from giving live, in-person presentations to groups of one hundred to one thousand people. I'd typically speak for regional and national conferences of large professional associations. I also did some work in the corporate world and schools. It was rare that I spoke to a group smaller than fifty people.

As I returned to the office that Monday morning, the emails and calls started pouring in immediately. Clients were unsure of this new development's impact on their events. It was starting to sound as though large gatherings of people may be ill-advised, and they were understandably hedging their bets. Some cancelled their events outright, and most postponed indefinitely. In the space of five days, my projected revenue for the year went from six figures to zero. That is not hyperbole. By 5:00 p.m. on Friday, I had $0 coming on the next paycheque and, what was worse, it seemed unlikely I'd be able to work for the foreseeable future.

What do you do when it feels like your world is collapsing around you? When you're surrounded by chaos and confusion and feel like every option available to you is unappealing, how do you move forward? Your life and your work can change quickly and dramatically, sometimes without warning. Is it possible to prepare ourselves for these inevitable but often unpredictable challenges? Yes, it is. The Resilience Roadmap Framework™ is a detailed, step-by-step action plan for thinking and behaving your way through all the challenges you face at work and at home.

WHO IS THIS BOOK FOR?

If you're reading these words, that already says a lot. You were attracted enough to the title to buy this book. Now you've made it through the first few pages and you're still reading. That, too, is a good indication that this book is probably for you. But in case you're still not sure, if you chose your career or vocation because you love it or want to make an impact and help other people in some way, this book is for you.

Nurses, teachers, social workers, and the like, this book is for you. However, it's also for executives, salespeople, and professionals. I wrote this book for anyone who finds themself stuck between their desire to serve the people they care about and a system or bureaucracy that too often restricts how they do that. If that's you, you're in the right place, and I have to tell you that I have great admiration for you. I deeply respect what you do and why you do it. It would be easy to go do something different—something with fewer demands and less stress, anxiety, and frustration. It would be easier to go somewhere where you could punch the clock and leave your work at work every night.

Yes, that would be easier. But then again, you aren't interested in easy; you're interested in what matters. You do what you do because at some level you hope you can make the world around you just a little bit better because of what you do. But there's a problem, isn't there? Because most of the time things don't work the way they're supposed to. Counter to the optimistic vision you had for your career, the reality is often far different. You've learned with time and experience that the demands always seem to exceed your time and energy. You're perpetually overextended and under-resourced.

Despite how clear it is to you and your colleagues that things need to change, the powers that be continue failing to make the hard decisions necessary for creating real results. They talk a good game, but when push comes to shove, they make decisions that create short-term wins in exchange for long-term failure. Increasingly you don't just feel unsupported, you feel like you're being actively thwarted, as though the very people who are supposed to ensure you have everything you need to help those you serve are actively making things harder for you.

If that were the only problem, maybe it would be manageable. But the bigger problem is that these challenges don't end when you leave work. Your daily reality is that you almost always seem to run out of hours before you run out of items on your to-do list; your energy runs out before your day does. The idealistic world-changer you saw in the mirror as you began your career has been replaced by someone you barely recognize. Someone getting by. Someone who too often is going through the motions rather than living with intention and purpose. Someone who ends their days collapsing in a heap and greets their alarm with a sense of mild dread.

Does that sound familiar? If even half of those words ring true to you, this book is for YOU. By the end of these pages, you'll have not only a systematic framework for coping with the increasingly challenging and complex world in which you find yourself, but a renewed confidence in your capacity to thrive no matter what challenges come your way.

A WORD ABOUT YOUR "BOAT"

Before we continue, I think it's important to clarify that resilience is complex. It's influenced by how we think and act, but it's also impacted by our history, our culture, and our access to resources. Certainly, no one is immune to hardship or obstacles, but it's undeniable that we each bring a different set of tools to the table. It would be an oversimplification to suggest that everyone is equally equipped to cope with the multitude of obstacles life presents. I want to be clear from the outset of this book, as I invite you to strengthen your mind and help you develop better strategies for facing challenges and change, I recognize each of us faces those challenges with a different toolbox.

Near the start of the COVID-19 pandemic, I saw a social media post that expressed a critical insight about coping with challenges and change. There's an expression familiar to most of us that says, "We are all in the same boat," meaning that everyone is in this together and no one is unaffected. The social media post I saw, however, gave a new twist to the expression that clarified an important distinction. To paraphrase, it said something like, "We are NOT all in the same boat. We are all in the same storm, but we are sailing in different boats."

Even during a global pandemic that impacted the entire world, there was still a significant range of experiences within that universality. Just because we were all facing the same virus doesn't mean we were all facing the same reality. Those of us in wealthy countries had the support of robust healthcare systems. We had first access to vaccines when they were developed. Many of us had the luxury of choosing whether to work from home or continue going in to work with PPE and other protective measures.

This is not to suggest that the experience was easy for anyone. Clearly, that's not the case. However, we can't deny that it was easier to face COVID-19 with all those resources than it must've been for people in remote villages in Africa. There, people depend on close contact with each other for survival, and vaccines were only accessible by walking to clinics miles away—if they were accessible at all. No, we were not in the same boat at all.

In this book, you'll read about some of my personal and professional challenges. I share them mostly because it's in living through these experiences that I discovered and codified the principles of the Resilience Roadmap Framework. My intention is that they will serve as useful illustrations of how you can apply the framework to yourself and your particular situation.

Depending on your life experiences, my examples may appear to be significantly greater or rather minuscule compared to yours. Resist the temptation to measure your experiences against mine (or anyone else's). It will never be an apples-to-apples comparison anyway. While I've faced some significant challenges in my life, I've also been blessed with many resources and sociological advantages. I was born in Canada to two married, well-educated parents, both with good jobs and stable family backgrounds. There's no history of addiction or abuse in my family. The parents of both of my parents were each married until the day they died (over fifty years each), and my parents have been married for over forty years as well.

If you're familiar with sociological data on those particular variables, you know that I essentially won the birth lottery. In other words, I've faced some intense storms, but I've been fortunate that my boat was well-equipped.

So as you read this book, please know that I have great compassion for you if you don't find yourself in that same situation. You may feel like you have no support. You may feel gravely under-resourced to handle what life is throwing at you. For that, I can only say I empathize. My hope is that the tools in this book will provide you with enough resources to make it. Perhaps it won't be as easy for you as for someone else. Unfortunately, such is life. Each of us reaches a point in our lives where we must decide whether the challenges we've faced and the resources we've been deprived of will define us or refine us. Will we allow these factors to limit what we can do and who we can become? Or will we accept the hand we have been dealt and focus our efforts on playing each card well? That's a choice we each get to make.

Change is never going away. In fact, it seems to be increasing in degree and frequency. The goal isn't to calm the storm but to ensure our boats are as well-equipped as possible. So let's start building your boat.

THE AGE OF UNCERTAINTY

> *"Faith is a place of mystery, where we find the courage to believe in what we cannot see and the strength to let go of our fear of uncertainty."*
>
> **–Brene Brown**, *The Gifts of Imperfection*

A s you read this, the world around us is changing at an ever-quickening pace. From technology to the environment, science to the arts, everything and everyone are changing all the time, and there's every reason to believe the pace of change will only increase. Uncertainty and instability are commonplace, and things that were once considered impossible happen with regularity. If ever there was a time in history when it was important to be able to adjust to a variety of changing situations, it is now.

You can probably remember a time that seemed simpler than today. A time when it felt like things moved a little slower and you had more answers to more of life's problems. I know I certainly feel that way sometimes. Whether that perception is accurate or we're simply looking at the past through rose-coloured glasses, as can often be the case, doesn't matter. We can't go back. The very idea of "the good old days" is dubious but, more importantly, irrelevant. We can't go back in time no matter how much we might think we want to. The only option we have, whether we like it or not, is to find a way to move forward. The only real question is how. Will we move forward in our careers and lives with optimism and enthusiasm, or fear and anxiety?

To be sure, there's plenty to be concerned about. We're facing an impending environmental disaster. The writing is on the wall. Only those who are determined to deny it can ignore that our planet is in dire need of massive intervention. We're already seeing the effects: dramatic temperature increases and fluctuations, rising water levels, melting ice caps, and species extinction are just a few of the warning signs that we are on a crash course with disaster. Credible scientists are unanimous in their prediction that climate change will have an ever-increasing impact on how and where we live.

Change isn't new. Since the dawn of man, things have always been changing and evolving. What has changed recently, however, is the scope and rate of that change. Circumstances are evolving to greater degrees and at a much greater pace than in the past, and this trend doesn't show signs of slowing down. Imagine if someone who died in 1972 came back to Earth today.

Think of the changes that have occurred in just the last fifty years. Fifty years ago, we were just getting used to having a television, and it had only a few channels. We had telephones that sat on the wall and were attached to a cord, analog watches, and cars that ran on diesel gas. That was about the extent of the technology available at the time. Though we managed to put a man on the moon, the computers NASA required to complete the first lunar mission took up several rooms. Today we have smart HD televisions and computers on our wrists and in our pockets that are more powerful than those NASA used to launch the rocket that went to the moon. And over 2.6 billion people on the planet have a smartphone, according to an article on TechCrunch.[1]

Fifty years ago, our world was also confined to our town or region. Most people didn't travel extensively because it was inconvenient and expensive. The internet and social media have connected the global community in ways we previously could never have imagined. Now we can post a message, and in seconds someone on the other side of the planet can read it. How the information age will continue to impact the way we work and live remains to be revealed, but there's no question the changes will continue. However, this technological progress brings challenges of its own.

We are on the new frontier of artificial intelligence, which is already impacting more aspects of more people's lives. No longer the domain of science fiction, the day when robots do many things that currently require human intelligence is not far off. What will that mean for human civilization? How will it affect society? As people increasingly move toward online interactions, and with developments of such concepts as the metaverse, how long will it be before some people live more of their lives in a virtual reality than a physical one? What does that mean for society as we know it? How can we effectively educate students and prepare them for the world when we don't even know what the world will look like when they're done with school? How do we continue to effectively care for and support

---

[1] Ingrid Lunden, "6.1B Smartphone Users Globally By 2020, Overtaking Basic Fixed Phone Subscriptions," TechCrunch, June 2, 2015, https://techcrunch.com/2015/06/02/6-1b-smartphone-users-globally-by-2020-overtaking-basic-fixed-phone-subscriptions/.

a population whose average age is expected to increase significantly in the next decade?

Many of these big questions will affect us, yet we'll have very little influence or control over what happens. Paying attention is important, but needlessly worrying about the details when they're out of our control serves little purpose. I mention them simply to provide context and evidence of the impetus for writing this book: I believe resilience will be the single most important and valuable skill set of the next century. What skilled trades were to the early twentieth century, and what knowledge and information were to the last two decades, resilience will be for the next quarter-century.

In this emotional environment, it's easy to feel helpless. It's easy to feel like the world is going to hell and there's nothing we can do. I've felt that way. I suspect you have too. I have children, and sometimes when I think about the world I've brought them into, it scares the heck out of me. But before I suggest you read this book about resilience, it might be a good idea to figure out whether resilience even matters to you, and if it does, why?

Resilience is the most critical skill of the twenty-first century because, in an age of continuous and dramatic change, the only solution is to be prepared for whatever may come next. We aren't very good at predicting the specifics of the changes we'll face. Just look at the last thirty years. In the '80s we believed acid rain and AIDS would lead to the end of the world. In the '90s the internet was going to run out of control and machines would take over. Y2K brought a whole new level of paranoia and fear, and we were sure that a single digit would cause a global catastrophe. In 2008 the financial meltdown had a massive impact worldwide, and many thought it would be the end of the global economy. We have survived all of it.

The reason we're still here is because human beings are fundamentally resilient. We survive. We find a way to get through whatever we have to get through. Science shows that we've been doing it for roughly two hundred thousand years. Over that time we've survived earthquakes, floods, and droughts. We've survived attacks from other species and our own. We've survived wars and conflicts. Despite all the threats that still exist, we have every reason to believe that we'll continue to survive for a long, long time. Why? Because of our incredible capacity for resilience.

For millennia we've been facing adversity and finding solutions. We've learned, reacted, adapted, and grown. But what if we could be more proactive? What if we didn't have to wait to react to what life threw at us but instead prepared ourselves in advance?

It's tempting to try to anticipate every possible scenario and eventuality and develop the solutions to solve them all. While that approach may be warranted in specific instances, on the whole the issues are too varied and too dramatic to anticipate them all and prepare for every potential problem. Rather than preparing every possible solution to every possible problem, we must instead focus on building our capacity to handle whatever may come our way.

You and I, as individual citizens, have virtually no control over the significant forces that impact our lives. Matters such as the economy, environment, and government are things we can have a say in, but they are certainly not things we control.

We won't always get the results we want in life. There are too many variables, and too many things are out of our control to hope to live a life in which we get what we want all the time. Resilience isn't about preventing failure and ensuring we always get what we want. That's impossible. Resilience is about effectively coping with our failures while enjoying life in the process.

So how can we do that?

If we can't stop it from raining, we need to make sure we take the time to buy an umbrella. That's what building resilience is all about.

We know it will rain. That's life. Bad things will happen. There will be job loss and career change. There will be relationship conflict and financial struggle. There will be illness and death. These things aren't in question; they're an inevitable part of life. The question is not "Will they happen?" but rather "WHEN will they happen?"

This is a good time to pause and define our terms of reference for this book. What does *resilience* mean in this context? Rather than bore you with dictionary definitions, let me advance my chosen definition while leaving room for you to find yours as you read the rest of these pages.

To me, resilience is the ability to adapt to, thrive in, and grow through challenge and change. That may not be exactly in line with what you've been taught resilience means. When I ask audiences to define what resilience is, I typically get answers such as "perseverance," "grit," and "determination." These are all important characteristics to be sure, but they are only parts of what it means to be resilient. Another popular definition is some version of "bouncing back from adversity." This definition is likely the most common, but it's also the one most fraught with problems.

Primarily, "bouncing back" is technically impossible. Think about it. The implication of "bouncing back" is that a person or organization faces a challenge or adversity, is metaphorically knocked down by it, and then somehow gets back up to return to a similar state as before the adversity struck. It sounds simple enough, except that isn't how resilience really works.

Think of any trial in your life. What is something you've experienced that challenges you in a significant way? Have you gone through a divorce, lost your job, faced a difficult medical diagnosis, or lost someone you loved deeply? Have you been bullied, struggled to fit in, or worried about how you were going to pay the rent? Of course you have. We've all faced challenges of varying degrees in our lives and work. It's an inescapable part of the human experience.

Whether you've overcome your challenge entirely or you're still walking through it, can you imagine your life ever being as it was before this adversity struck? Once you've lived through a divorce, will you ever look at relationships the same way? If you've been on the brink of bankruptcy and managed to survive, do you look at money the same way you did before? If you've experienced a life-altering illness, do you see life with the same perspective you had before you got sick? Of course not. Every day we experience and learn things that impact who we are and how we see the world. Often the impact is quite small, other times it's significant, but you're not the same person you were this time last year, and neither am I. So why are we trying to "bounce back?" We can't return to the person we used to be any more than we can rewind the calendar and relive 2020 (not that anyone wants to do that).

So if resilience isn't about "bouncing back," what *is* it about? It's about growing through challenge and change. Since we know that challenge and change are never going away and that time will never stand still, our only option is to keep moving. The question is, will you be a better person tomorrow than you were today? Will you let the challenges you face make you better or make you bitter?

Those who are resilient don't just *survive* life's challenges, they *thrive* through them. Whether it's the Great Depression, the market crash in 1987, the dot com bubble burst, or the COVID-19 pandemic, resilient people and resilient organizations don't simply survive challenging times, they leverage the changes and challenges they face to make them better. That's what I want for you. The Resilience Roadmap Framework is specifically designed to help you think and act through whatever you're facing right now and whatever will come next.

WHY SHOULD YOU LISTEN TO ME?

"The only source of knowledge is experience."

—Albert Einstein

I 've been speaking and writing since 2003. Despite the years that have passed since then, I can still vividly remember how insecure I was at that time—insecure not only about myself, as I think all young people are, but about my worthiness to stand on a stage and speak.

When someone is hired as a speaker to address any group of people, there's an onus to present something useful; or at least there should be. Whether it's sharing stories that motivate and inspire or teaching information that educates or imparts a skill, a speaker should leave their audience with something valuable to take away.

When I gave my first presentation, I didn't think I could do either of those things.

I was twenty-five years old and had recently returned home from a harrowing year of health struggles, which I'll share in detail later in this chapter. Since I come from a small town, the local paper reported my ordeal. Maybe that's why a local high school principal invited me to speak at her upcoming graduation ceremony. She asked me to share some of my story and whatever I had learned that might be helpful to the three hundred seventeen- and eighteen-year-old graduates and their families who would be in attendance.

With the help of my mom and a few other people, I pieced together a ten-minute presentation I hoped would be helpful in some way while being fully aware that these graduates would have little interest in what I had to say. After all, I would be one of the last things standing between them and the parties and celebrations they'd attend after the graduation ceremony.

I don't remember much of what I said that evening. I know I got a few chuckles from the students, which was gratifying, but I wasn't sure I had imparted any wisdom. However, at the reception after the ceremony, I had an encounter that transformed my life and set me on a path that ultimately led to my writing this book. The following recount is paraphrased based on my memory.

One of the parents approached me at the reception and, after sharing a few kind words about my presentation, asked me for my business card. While it was a simple and straightforward request, I was genuinely confused by it. I'd recently landed my first "real job" in an entry-level position at an insurance company and didn't have a business card. As I tried to grasp what this man was asking for, I finally mumbled something about not having a card and asked him why he wanted one from me. "Well, *that* is what you do, right?" he asked, pointing at the stage where I had delivered my speech.

I was still confused. "People do that as a job?" I asked.

"Yes. We bring people into my company to do what you just did, and I think we pay them quite well," he responded.

A lightbulb went off. Could I actually share my story and what I learned from it? Could I help people by doing that? Could I actually earn a living delivering speeches?

It took less than a year before I gave my first "professional" speech. I spoke to a few hundred students in a school gymnasium and was paid $100. A humble beginning to say the least, yet it was proof to me that people might actually pay money to hear what I had to say. For the next three years, I worked my regular job from 8:30–4:30 and spent the evenings online doing research about how to become a professional speaker. The following year, I left the job at the insurance company and began working as a substitute teacher. This job paid about the same but allowed me the flexibility to take a day off if I managed to book a presentation. Two years later, I was making almost as much money as a part-time speaker as I was in my teaching job. After consulting my wife, I decided to try to make speaking my full-time career. That was in 2008. The rest, as they say, is history.

In the years since that first speech to elementary students, I've travelled the continent from Newfoundland to Hawaii teaching this book's framework to hundreds of organizations, including Exxon Mobil, Sunlife Financial, and the Million Dollar Round Table.

The Resilience Roadmap Framework in this book works. As you'll see in the following chapters, research and data from a variety of studies back up everything you'll read. Interestingly, however, the framework isn't the result of research at all. It's the result of reverse engineering my lived experiences, particularly from the seventeen months between July 2000 and December 2002. In the next few pages, I provide an abridged version of the events that ultimately led me to write this book. My hope is that it will provide context for the origin of the Resilience Roadmap and earn your confidence that what you're about to read isn't just a theory, but a battle-tested formula for effectively coping with adversity and change.

THE ORIGIN STORY

Bill and Monique Black were like any young, newly married couple: they were in love and anxious to welcome their first child into the world. Like any soon-to-be parents, the usual anxieties and concerns were there, but there was no way they could properly prepare for what was about to happen. Without the advantages of advanced ultrasound, there was no way for Monique and Bill to know that the birth of their firstborn son would begin a journey that would change their lives.

Monique went into labour on May 8, 1978, and as soon as her son was delivered, it was clear something wasn't right. The baby began turning blue. Rather than enjoying that first beautiful moment of life holding their newborn son in their arms, Monique and Bill were forced to watch helplessly as their child was quickly rushed away in a sea of nurses and doctors.

They waited hours as doctors worked to stabilize their infant son and diagnose the problem. Finally, the doctors returned and gave Bill and Monique news they could never have prepared for: their son needed open-heart surgery to repair a closed aortic valve. He would be flown by helicopter to the children's hospital in a few hours.

Can you imagine it? I can't. As a parent of three, I can't imagine how I'd deal with watching my son being flown away for emergency surgery, not knowing whether I'd see him alive again. The sheer uncertainty would be overwhelming.

A few hours later, Monique and Bill watched out the window as their son was flown to the Isaak Walton Killam Hospital for

Children in Halifax, Nova Scotia, where he would undergo open-heart surgery to open his aortic valve. They were forced to wait for Monique to recover before following their son to Halifax.

Fortunately, the gifted surgeons and staff were able to save my life that day. Against the odds, the doctors were able to open the valve, allowing my heart to properly supply oxygenated blood to my tiny body. However, I was far from out of the woods. The recovery was months long, and less than a year later there was another surgery to repair the aorta, the main artery of the heart.

Again blessed, with a great surgeon and phenomenal medical care, I survived, but at this point it was clear to my parents that they wouldn't have a normal life with their son. Doctors had no clear predictions for what would happen next, but they warned Bill and Monique that it could be a tough journey.

I was fortunate. The doctors predicted the valve would need attention again soon, but it didn't. They assumed another surgery would be required before I started school and that my health may negatively impact my schooling, causing me to graduate late—if I was indeed lucky enough to live that long. By God's grace, the doctors were wrong. My childhood was full of doctor's appointments and hospital visits, but my health remained stable. Not only did I live, but I was able to keep up in school and even compete in sports.

For the first thirteen years of my life, I thought I was pretty normal. I was significantly shorter than the other kids, and I had this long scar that ran down the front of my chest, but besides that I lived a normal life and felt like a very normal kid.

In truth I was anything but normal. Even as a child I was followed closely by doctors. I had semi-annual check-ups at the Izaak Walton Killam Hospital to monitor my heart condition and adjust medications. In a typical year I'd be hospitalized with asthma at least once. The whole time we knew that one day, at some point, the non-invasive medical options to keep my heart working would run out and we'd be forced to face the last available intervention—a heart transplant.

It would've been very easy, understandable, and even, some would argue, the most responsible thing to do for my parents to protect me carefully. They could've put me in the proverbial bubble and tried to prevent anything bad from happening to me. After all, I was sick. I had a congenital, chronic health condition. It would seem the responsible thing to do would be to keep me inside and the world outside. But my parents didn't do that.

Bill and Monique were both physical education teachers. They were trained in health and the benefits of physical activity and sport. I don't know whether it was that background or God that gave them some special insight and wisdom that the average twenty-three-year-old, first-time parent doesn't have, but they made a conscious decision very early in my life to do the exact opposite of what may have seemed like the logical thing.

A wise nurse told Mom early on that the best way to help me feel like a normal kid would be to treat me like one. Mom and Dad had witnessed the effects that coddling had on the other patients I shared rooms with over the first few years. They could see how they were more anxious and dependent than their peers. They could see how these kids were not properly equipped to deal with the "real world" outside of the hospital walls. As teachers, they had taught these kids. The ones who were afraid to try new things or to scrape their knees. The ones who would cry when they lost a game or when someone treated them in any way other than how they expected.

Hospitalization during childhood also forces early maturation. At a young age, when other kids are playing with their friends, sick children are spending a lot more time with adults. They're having very "grown up" conversations about very serious issues—ones that a young child shouldn't have to deal with. While that can cause some to mature much more quickly, it can cause others to retreat into their shell and not mature much at all. These children become dependent on their parents, in large part because they feel powerless over their lives.

Mom and Dad were vigilant in ensuring I wouldn't become one of those kids. They made it a point never to shelter me from the truth about my health. I learned about every new development in my health situation—good or bad—straight from the doctors' lips. In an attempt to protect their child, many parents talked to the doctors without their sick child present. They filtered the news and shared only what they deemed appropriate for their child to hear. My parents knew that someday I'd have to be responsible for my own health, which would require practice. So from a very young age, I was there when the doctors talked to us about whatever was happening.

So when my condition deteriorated early in my teen years, I learned about it first-hand. I was in the room when the cardiologist explained I was in atrial fibrillation, a condition in which the top chambers of the heart no longer contract properly. The condition itself isn't fatal, but it increases the risk of several potentially fatal events such as arrhythmia, stroke, and cardiac arrest.

As the son of two physical education teachers, I participated in a variety of sports throughout my childhood. My two favourites were basketball and soccer. I played at a competitive level despite always being the shortest boy on the team. What I lacked in size, I made up for in competitive spirit and hard work. I loved to play. I loved to compete. It was exactly that intense competitiveness that caused concern for my doctors. They were worried that if a cardiac event happened during a game, I'd likely try to push through the symptoms until it was too late. Allowing me to continue playing was simply too risky. I was encouraged to stay active by doing light exercise such as walking, but competitive sports had to stop.

I was crushed. The field and the court were the places I felt most valuable as a thirteen-year-old boy. I had skills many of my friends didn't, and being part of a team and contributing to that team meant the world to me. Without that, I had no idea what I would do.

It took me nearly a year to find another outlet for myself. I needed a way to have those same experiences of belonging and contributing. I needed a way to share my gifts and talents and feel like I was a part of something special. I found it in drama and theatre. No longer being able to play sports forced me toward new and interesting places. I tried out for drama club in middle school and learned I had some ability. I was cast in a few plays and even won an award at our small theatre festival.

Throughout high school and university, the theatre and the stage—not sports and a field—were where I was able to shine. It's no doubt my experience in theatre, which allowed me to perform in front of several hundred, sometimes even a thousand people, prepared me for my career today as a professional speaker. From the day of my very first speech, I didn't have the nerves of being in front of people that most do. I was used to it.

The experiences I gained in the theatre have given me the confidence to perform in this new way. It's much more vulnerable to stand on a stage and share your own story than it is to tell someone else's. It's a very different thing to be yourself in front of a thousand people than it is to play a character. After all, if I play a character and the audience doesn't like it, I can blame the character, the playwright, the other actors, or the director. But when I'm standing alone on stage sharing *me* and people don't like it, there's only one person to blame: myself.

Why do I share those stories with you? Because it's imperative to understand that if we want to build our resilience capacity, facing adversity is non-negotiable. We can't learn to swim by learning about swimming, watching swimming videos, or reading about swimming techniques. We can't learn to ride a bike simply by watching other people ride a bike. We have to do it ourselves. We have to get in the water and struggle to stay afloat, and we have to get on the bike, fall off, and get back on again.

The trials I faced as a child, and the decisions my parents made to not shelter or overprotect me from them, provided a great opportunity. They allowed me to get equipped. I was able to acquire the necessary tools, strategies, and attitudes I'd need for what would come next.

My health challenges didn't end at thirteen. In fact, they only grew in severity and complexity. A decade later I would face a much greater obstacle than the end of my athletic pursuits. I would face the end of my life. I'll share the details of that story in another chapter, but suffice it to say for now, my trials of infancy and childhood served to prepare me well for what would happen in adolescence and adulthood.

THE FRAMEWORK

When was the last time you thought about your car's spare tire? I'm going to go out on a limb and guess it's been a very long time, if you can even remember a time at all. Am I right? Much like we don't think much about the spare tire on our car until we get a flat (do you even know where to find the spare tire in your car?), we don't think about our ability to be resilient until we face a situation that requires us to be.

In the spring of 2020, everyone in the world was given a powerful reminder of the importance of resilience skills. As flights were grounded, the economy was shut down, and people were sent home from work, the reality set in that nothing is immune to disruption. When you witness how something as simple as a virus can grind the world to a halt in a matter of weeks, it's impossible to deny that the fragility of every aspect of our lives can be flipped on its head. Here's the problem: when you need to call on your resilience, it's too late. If you wait until you need the spare tire to find out that you don't have one, it's too late.

According to the Life Insurance Marketing and Research Association, 106 million adults lack life insurance or adequate coverage.[2] Of those who did have coverage, nearly half had less than $100,000 worth of coverage, which in most experts' opinions isn't nearly enough. It's a scary and fascinating thing to know that we're all going to die. One of the few guarantees in life is that one day it will end. If we know that something is definitely going to happen, and we know that thing will cost money—money we may not have—why wouldn't we insure against that risk? It's actually not hard to understand when you consider basic human psychology. As a rule, we tend to be short-term thinkers. We'd rather have something now than later. This tendency is part of the explanation for a variety of human ills, from obesity to global warming. The ability to delay gratification now for the sake of a greater good later is something we all struggle with. Given that struggle, it's no wonder so many people choose to have more money in their pocket today than ensure their loved ones have enough money to bury them, let alone pay off the house or replace their income.

The same short-sightedness is at play when it comes to working on our resilience. Why, you may ask, should you work on developing a skill you don't need right now?

---

[2] "Life Insurance Awareness Month (2022)," LIMRA, accessed December 14, 2022, https://www.limra.com/en/newsroom/liam/.

Just as death is a certainty, your eventual need to be resilient is one of life's guarantees. I've never met a single person on the planet who has never faced a challenge. No matter your age, I'm certain you don't have to look back very far into your past to think of the last difficult challenge you had to face. You may be facing one right now. It may be why you bought this book.

If you know for sure that you will face challenges in your life and that being more resilient is the key to coping with those challenges in a more productive way, then why wouldn't you want to proactively build your "resilience factor" now? You can't buy home insurance after your house burns down. The time is now.

Obviously, you could choose to wait. You could choose to never prepare for challenges or not face them at all. But we both know that if it hasn't happened already in your life, at some point you'll be stretched to the brink. You'll be tested in ways you've never been tested before. I don't know about you, but I want to be ready when that happens to me next. I wasn't ready last time, and it was extremely difficult. I vowed to never let that happen to me again, and I don't want it to happen to you either. So let's get to work.

In this chapter, we're going to outline a complete framework for developing and deploying resilience in every area of your life. If you find yourself in a challenging situation, this is the map you can follow to navigate through it and come out the other side not only intact, but stronger, wiser, and better than you were before.

I present The Resilience Roadmap Framework as seven steps or guideposts. The framework is neat and tidy because that makes it easier for you to learn, digest, and apply the steps to your life and work. However, our lives and work are not strictly linear journeys. We don't go from point A, "the problem," to point B, "the solution," in a straight line, nor do we ever arrive at a point where the challenges and problems are over. We never reach a finish line until we breathe our last breath. Life continues moving forward, and so must we. So as you read through this framework, understand that you'll have to go back to previous steps many times in your life and your career.

The Resilience Roadmap™
7 Guideposts for Charting Your Course in a chaotic world.

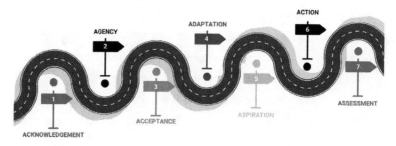

©2022 Resurgo Training Solutions Inc. All rights reserved.

As we go through this step-by-step process and read the examples provided, I invite you to think of a particularly challenging situation you've faced in your own life. See if you can spot which guideposts you used in dealing with that situation and which of them you may have omitted or glossed over too quickly. Were any of those guideposts the reason the challenge was harder than it needed to be? What would've changed if you had applied each of the following principles?

1. **Acknowledgement:** If this sounds obvious, that's because it should be. You can't solve a problem you're unwilling to face. The problem, of course, is that we often find ourselves doing everything we can to avoid dealing with an obvious issue that's staring us in the face. Maybe we think if we ignore the problem it will somehow solve itself. Maybe we simply aren't ready to

face the truth. Either way, unless and until we can look squarely at our challenges and face them head-on, we have no chance of dealing with them effectively. What are you dealing with? Are you seeing it accurately? Are you biassed toward the negative? Are you oversimplifying? Are you underestimating the challenges that lie ahead?

2. **Agency:** Resilience begins with a fundamental belief that we have the capacity to affect the outcomes in our lives. If your subconscious belief is that life happens *to* you, that you have no control over what happens, then there's no point in reading the rest of this book. You'll never be as resilient as you could be if you have a fundamental belief that you're powerless to change your circumstances. None of us can control everything (which is why you'll see that one of the guideposts of the framework is about acceptance), but we can always control certain aspects of every situation. You simply must believe that to be true, even if you don't always feel like it is. It's on that fundamental belief that the rest of the roadmap is built.

3. **Acceptance:** We live immersed in a culture of self-determination. We're told repeatedly—even in books like this one—that we are the masters of our destiny; we ought to be able to control all the outcomes in our work and our lives, or so say many personal development gurus. We have significant influence over what happens to us and should do whatever we can to give ourselves and those we care about the best opportunity to succeed. However, the reality is that there are still many parts of our work and personal lives over which we have no control. I could list dozens of examples, but after the global pandemic of COVID-19, I suspect that's not necessary. If we learned one thing between 2020 and 2022, it was that no matter how much we plan and prepare, no matter how good our habits are, and no

matter how well we execute our plans, we simply can't control everything in our lives. So the question then becomes, Can you let go of the things you can't control?

Many of us are held back less by the real obstacles in our path than by our desperate attempts to try to manipulate every circumstance of our lives. When we try to hang onto control of everything knowing full well that it's impossible to do, we exhaust our most precious and finite resources: our time and our energy. To be resilient, we must learn to let go of what we can't control so that we have the resources at our disposal to control the things we can.

4. **Adaptation:** The world changes quickly. Often our days don't unfold exactly as planned and we're forced to make adjustments large and small. Adaptability is an essential skill for all of us to develop. My prediction is it will become increasingly important in the coming years. Being as resilient as possible means not only adapting when necessary but doing so proactively, willingly, and with as little resistance as possible. How do you need to change your ways of thinking and behaving so you can function at your best in this new world? What old ways of thinking and being do you need to challenge and change?

5. **Aspiration:** Resilience is typically framed as a reactive process. Some significant event occurs that knocks us down, and then we have to be resilient to recover. However, one of the essential elements of being resilient is hope. To be truly resilient, we must be able to sustain our efforts of adaptation and change over a significant period of time, and the way to do that is by having a fundamental belief that tomorrow can be better than today. Sustaining our efforts is much easier when we know we're moving toward something worthwhile, and that requires us to build a clear and compelling vision for the future.

What do you want? Can you envision a future better than today? What kind of life do you want to create? What is your purpose or mission? Can you see it? A clear and compelling vision of a better future is the most powerful driver of action.

6. **Action:** There's nothing complicated about this step, but it's the place where many people fail. All the theorizing and planning in the world don't amount to anything unless we do something about the challenges we face. Having a clear and compelling vision for the future is important, but that future will never come to be if we don't take significant action. Many people wait for the world to conform to them. They hope to stumble into the reality they want instead of proactively trying to create it. Don't be that person. We can't expect that simply wishing things were different will make it so. We have to actually do something.

    The good news is that our actions don't necessarily need to be big. In fact, massive action is hard to sustain. Typically the most resilient people are those who execute small, consistent efforts over a long period of time.

7. **Assessment:** Have you ever mistakenly taken a wrong turn and driven for miles in the wrong direction before realizing it? It's a frustrating feeling to know that you've wasted time and energy going the wrong way. This is why it's so important to periodically take the time to assess where we are and where we're going. We need to create feedback loops to ensure we're on the right track. If we find we aren't, we can adjust and begin again.

That's it. The seven guideposts to becoming more resilient. Simple, though not easy. These are the principles and strategies I've used to go from my deathbed to the finish line of marathons. They are the principles and strategies I used when COVID-19 eviscerated my business and I had to rebuild it from scratch. They are the principles and strategies I've shared with hundreds of organizations to help them navigate through tumultuous times. And they are the principles and strategies that will help you thrive in the face of whatever adversity you meet.

We are never going to be able to stop it from raining, but we can ensure that we have a nice big umbrella to use when it does. Are you ready to build your umbrella? Are you ready to increase your capacity to proactively handle whatever adversity you face? Let's go.

ACKNOWLEDGEMENT

*"When we least expect it, life sets us a challenge to test
our courage and willingness to change; at such a moment,
there is no point in pretending that nothing has happened
or in saying that we are not yet ready. The challenge will
not wait. Life does not look back."*

—Paulo Coelho

It was May of 2001. I had just finished the first of a two-year
Bachelor of Education program and was well on my way to ful-
filling my long-stated intention of becoming a teacher like my parents. From the outside looking in, everything was great. Life was
progressing according to plan, and in another year I'd begin my
adult life in a rewarding career I was passionate about. I could hardly
ask for better in most respects, yet something was amiss.

For several months I'd been feeling off. Nearly all of my classes
were held in the same building on campus, which was at the top of

a long, rather steep hill. Every day I walked up the hill to go to class and back down to come home. Over the course of the second semester, the walk to class started becoming more difficult. I found myself stopping halfway up the hill to catch my breath. Chalking it up to the cold weather of Canadian winters, I didn't think much of it. But by the end of the semester, the walk and breaks took even longer—if I even walked at all; often, I had my friend drive me instead. I was also eating less and feeling generally fatigued, despite getting a good night's sleep the night before.

As I look back now, it seems inconceivable that I didn't recognize something was seriously wrong. Several red flags during those months should've prompted me to seek medical advice. After all, I had spent the entirety of my twenty-plus years of life in and out of hospitals. I knew more about my body than most people do, and I knew that my heart condition had been slowly deteriorating for years. It should've been blatantly obvious that what I was experiencing were signs of trouble, and I should've sought medical advice. But for months, I didn't. I ignored, I rationalized, and I employed a variety of coping mechanisms to pretend that everything was okay, even though at some level I knew it wasn't.

At this same time, I received confirmation that I had landed a coveted summer job. Any university student would tell you that getting a job as a parliamentary tour guide in Ottawa is one of the best summer jobs a student could hope for. It was a chance to live in another city, learn about Canadian history, meet other students from across the county, and make good money doing a job that was relatively easy. On top of all of that, my girlfriend of the last three years, the woman I thought I might marry, had moved back to her hometown of Ottawa the year we graduated undergrad. We'd been dating long distance for the last year, and now I was going to get to spend the summer with her. I was over the moon.

When the school year ended a few weeks later, I came home to see my parents, pack my bags, and head off for a summer adventure. In retrospect, I think both my parents and I had some concerns that I wasn't one hundred percent healthy, but the excitement for this once-in-a-lifetime experience overcame any concerns I had, and I convinced myself and my parents that I was ready to move to Ottawa. A week or so later, I left to begin training for my new job.

Within a few weeks of arriving, I knew I had made a mistake. The fatigue I'd been experiencing off and on for months grew more frequent and more intense. My belly started to swell and feel uncomfortable. I found it increasingly difficult to sustain even short amounts of exercise, and I had little to no appetite. Something was seriously wrong, and now I was scared. I made the difficult decision to tell my new boss that I was going to go home to see my doctors and find out what was going on.

When I arrived home and my mom saw me, reality set in quickly. Her jaw dropped. She couldn't believe how I looked. "You have lost a lot of weight," she said with great concern in her voice. I was sure she was overreacting, but I agreed to weigh myself to assure her I was fine. I walked upstairs, entered the bathroom, and stood on the scale. I was shocked. The number on the scale read 87 lb.! To be fair, I'm a very small person. I'm 5'0" (okay, technically I'm 4'11", but with shoes on, I'm 5'0"). Even so, at a healthy weight I should be somewhere between 115 and 125 lb. I had lost roughly twenty pounds in a very short time span, and since twenty pounds represented more than fifteen percent of my body weight, it was a significant amount. Now, when I look back at pictures of myself, I can hardly believe I ever looked so frail and thin. But as is often the case in life, when things deteriorate slowly, they're easy to ignore.

When we saw that number on the scale, I agreed with my mom that I needed to get checked out by my doctor. I've been fortunate to have great physicians my entire life, but Dr. Laughlin was the best of them all. He'd been our family physician since I was a toddler. He knew my health intimately, so when he saw me that day, he didn't even need to complete his exam before deciding to admit me to the hospital. He immediately knew I was in congestive heart failure, a condition in which a failing heart causes fluid to back up into the lungs, making it harder to breathe. I was first admitted to a hospital where I lived in Moncton, but when doctors recognized that the situation was serious, I was transported by ambulance to Halifax to be evaluated by a team specializing in heart failure.

I stayed in the hospital in Halifax for a month while doctors ran a battery of tests to better understand exactly what was happening and what, if anything, could be done. Finally, in June of 2001, my cardiologist met with me to give me the results of their findings.

"Mark, you need a heart and double-lung transplant, and you need it now."

I will never forget those words. I never realized until that moment how one sentence could change a person's life.

That day, I was given a choice between two very difficult options. The first was to find a transplant centre that would consider having an eighty pound, twenty-four-year-old man with a lifetime of chronic illness on their transplant waiting list. My doctor told me that the odds of that happening were minuscule. Organs were hard to come by under the best of circumstances, and my circumstances were far from ideal.

Several things were working against me:

1. I needed three organs, not just one. Low donor rates meant that the "supply" of organs was nowhere near meeting the demand, and three organs were certainly harder to find than one.

2. Survival rates of transplants vary significantly by organ type. While a kidney transplant recipient could expect to live up to twenty to twenty-five years with a good match, the five-year survival rate for a lung transplant was less than fifty percent.

3. The fact that I had a congenital illness—that I was born with a heart problem—meant that statistically, even if the miraculous happened and a suitable donor was found, I was less likely to survive the surgery than someone who had been healthy most of their life.

The odds were clearly not in our favour.

Given that the odds of a successful heart and double-lung transplant in my situation were virtually zero, the second option was to consider returning home to preserve some quality of life for whatever time I had left. I was told that was likely two years at most.

I knew immediately what I wanted to do. I was not prepared to go home and wait to die. I would do whatever was necessary to get on a transplant list.

Since I'm writing this book twenty years later, you know how this story turns out. But it was far from easy, and there were several points in the journey where I didn't think I'd make it. I'll share more details of the journey in the pages ahead. I've often wondered whether I could've pushed the need for a transplant years into the future and spared myself significant suffering simply by being willing to acknowledge that something was wrong when I first felt the symptoms. What if I hadn't denied the obvious for so long? What if I had found the courage and honesty to face my health challenges head-on when the situation was less dire and more manageable? How would things have been different?

It's fascinating to me how easy it can be to look at events in our lives retrospectively and clearly see things we couldn't see at the time. It's similarly easy to look at someone else's situation and quickly identify what's wrong. Yet when it comes to our own lives, we often struggle to see the forest through the trees. Or is the problem not so much that we are *unable* to see but that we *choose* not to?

Freud posited that denial is our way of protecting the ego. If reality is painful, or if it's just uncomfortable enough that it challenges our ego, we will deny reality rather than face it. Today, some psychologists suggest that denial is far more nuanced than that; denial is perhaps even essential for us to get through daily living. Michael McCullough, a psychologist at the University of Miami and the author of *Beyond Revenge: The Evolution of the Forgiveness Instinct*, says that denial is the unspoken deal we make with ourselves and with others to get through our lives.[3]

We experience this denial every time we choose not to acknowledge a problem. Have you ever put off looking at a credit card statement? I know I have. Who hasn't felt like they were gaining some extra pounds but decided not to get on the scale? We know that refusing to open the envelope or log in to the computer doesn't make the debt go away, yet we choose to not look—just like I chose to pretend my health was fine despite all the signs that something was wrong.

As I'm writing this, I'm sitting in an airport lounge waiting for a flight to an event. It's 12:45 in the afternoon. Sitting to my right are two couples who appear to be heading off on a vacation together. They seem friendly enough, but they're speaking incredibly loudly and seem to be totally oblivious to the fact that they're bothering people around them. In fact, they're speaking so loudly that it's impossible not to hear their conversation.

---

[3] Benedict Carey, "Denial Makes the World Go Round," *New York Times*, November 20, 2007, https://www.nytimes.com/2007/11/20/health/20iht-20deni .8402176.html.

Not twenty minutes ago, one of the women was recounting a story in which someone she was with was drinking a lot. "Too much" was her characterization: "She had five drinks. That's too much." I'm fascinated, however, to notice that in the three hours I've been here, that same woman is on at least drink number six herself, and I have no idea what she may have consumed before I got here. Anyone who's been in an airport lounge knows this isn't uncommon. People drink and eat more than they normally would when it's free. I know I've certainly continued snacking even after I was full, simply because the food was there and free. So I pass no judgement on this woman or whether four drinks is "too much" for her in that span of time, but it's nonetheless telling that what she deemed "too much" for someone else less than an hour ago is now just fine for her. That's how easy it is to fail to acknowledge something when it may make us uncomfortable.

We all engage in self-deception to varying degrees, intentionally or otherwise. The only question is whether we admit to ourselves that sometimes we're either oblivious or intentionally dishonest with ourselves. Unless and until we do that, we have no hope of being as resilient as we could be.

Whenever we face an obstacle, challenge, or difficulty in our lives, the first thing we must do is acknowledge that it's there. Acknowledgement is more than simply noticing there's an issue. Yes, we certainly have to notice it, but we have to do more than that. Think of when you walk into a room and meet someone. Do you simply notice they are there, or do you really *acknowledge* them? Do you glance their way, or do you stop, look them in the eye, and maybe even chat?

Acknowledgement, then, is about more than simply noticing something is wrong. It's having the courage to face the situation and the self-awareness to admit how we're reacting to it so that we can then do something about it. We typically avoid acknowledging something out of fear, looking the other way hoping the problem will somehow take care of itself. Intellectually we already know this is a flawed strategy, but it provides momentary comfort. Avoidance and distraction are coping mechanisms that can work in the short term, but they ultimately cost you time, money, and energy. In the case of failing to acknowledge a health issue, it can even cost you your life.

Resilient people know the shortest route to getting through a challenge is walking straight through it. They don't shy away from obstacles and uncomfortable situations, because they know they'll eventually be forced to face them and prolonging the time until they do will likely make things worse.

Most children go through a phase of being afraid of the dark. Often they are sure that there are monsters lurking somewhere just out of sight in the closet or under the bed. Many parents have had to go into their child's room after putting them to bed and turn on the light to reassure their children that the shapes and shadows that appeared ominous in the dark are nothing to be afraid of.

While you have likely grown out of being afraid of literal darkness, we all still suffer to some degree from the fear of metaphorical darkness—fear of the unknown. The good news is, by simply turning on the metaphorical light—by acknowledging the situation—we can reduce or even eliminate our fears.

On March 8, 2020, I was sitting with my family in the Orlando airport. We were heading back home after enjoying a wonderful family vacation over spring break. As we waited for our plane, I noticed a headline on the news channel playing in the terminal. There was no volume, but the news ticker along the bottom of the screen was about a virus originating in China that was spreading across the globe. It was the first time I saw the word *coronavirus*.

Two days later, our local school board mandated that all students and teachers who'd been out of the country would have to quarantine for two weeks. We arrived home twenty-four hours before that cut-off, so my wife (who is a teacher) and my kids were all at school that week. Meanwhile, I sat in my home office fielding emails and phone calls from clients cancelling and postponing every speaking event on my calendar. By the end of the week, my entire income for the foreseeable future had disappeared. Suddenly I had no money coming in and, worse, no indication that I'd be able to earn any money as a speaker for the foreseeable future.

I was angry, frustrated, and confused. Most of all though, I was afraid. It was tempting to look away. It would've been much easier at that time to use avoidance or denial to cope. Thankfully, having made that mistake with my health situation and learning the hard lesson about the long-term cost of denial and avoidance, I took a metaphorical deep breath and faced reality. I didn't know what the future held or what exactly I would do, but I knew the shortest path to getting through this challenge was to walk straight through it.

It's important to acknowledge and recognize the challenges we face in life. Doing so allows us to better understand and address these challenges and can also help us feel more grounded and connected to our own experiences. Acknowledging your challenges doesn't mean that you're weak or flawed. On the contrary, it takes a great deal of courage and strength to confront and work through difficult situations. By acknowledging reality, you take an active role in your own growth and development and can work to create better results. Before moving on to the next guidepost, take some time to reflect on the following questions:

1. What situation or circumstance are you currently ignoring?
2. What do you need to face so that you can begin to address it?

3. How could ignoring that challenge make it worse?
4. What's one step to confront it that you can take before you go to bed tonight?

Remember that you're not alone in facing challenges and that there is support available to help you through difficult times. Seek out the help of friends, family, or professionals if you need it, and know that you have the strength and resilience to overcome any obstacle that comes your way.

At the conclusion of each of the chapters on the guideposts, I have included these reminders to reinforce the key learning points.

 RESILIENCE REMINDERS

- It is natural to use avoidance as a coping strategy for dealing with challenges and change, but it is a lousy strategy. If anything, it tends to make things worse.
- You cannot fix something unless you are first willing to admit it is an issue.
- By shining a light on our challenges we can reduce or even eliminate our fears and prepare ourselves to deal with them.

AGENCY

Once upon a time, a gentleman was walking through an elephant camp. He noticed the elephants were not kept in cages or held by chains and was shocked when he spotted that they were held only by a small piece of rope they could break very easily. The man was confused why the elephants were not using their strength to break the ropes and escape the camp. Curious to know, he went to the trainer and asked, "Why aren't they trying to escape the camp?"

The trainer replied, "When they are very young and much smaller, we use the same size rope to tie them and, at that age, it's enough to hold them. As they grow up, they are conditioned to believe they cannot break away. They believe the rope can still hold them, so they never try to break free."

The man was amazed to learn this. These animals could at any time break the rope and escape the camp, but because they believed it wasn't possible, they were stuck right where they were without trying to escape.[4]

How often in your life and work have you been like those elephants? Maybe some experiences in your childhood taught you that you were powerless. Maybe you've experienced significant failures in your life that have left you discouraged and defeated. Maybe you believe you aren't able to do anything about your situation; that whatever you do won't have an impact on the outcome, so you don't bother to try. I know I've fallen for this trap. It's all too easy to convince ourselves we are powerless over our circumstances. To be fair, there are absolutely aspects of our lives that are outside of our control. In fact, we'll delve into that in more detail in the next chapter. But we do have the power to use our failures to grow.

One of my favourite quotes comes from author and coach Marie Forleo who said, "Everything is *figureoutable*."[5] If you want to find success and fulfilment, if you want to not only overcome adversity but leverage it to your advantage in the form of personal growth, you must believe that it's possible. And not just possible for someone else, but possible for you. That sounds easy, but it's not. None of us are free from self-doubt. There's a good chance you're reading this right now with some level of hesitation. Sure it sounds good in theory, but can you really reach a point where you feel confident you can handle anything that comes your way? Yes, you can.

---

[4] Paraphrased from A. M. Marcus, *The Elephant and the Rope* (Scotts Valley, CA: CreateSpace Independent Publishing, 2015).

[5] Marie Forleo, *Everything is Figureoutable* (New York: Portfolio/Penguin, 2019).

The word *agency* has a few different meanings, but in the context of the Resilience Roadmap it's simply the word I use to describe your confidence in your ability to cope with whatever the world throws at you. This confidence is born from proof; the only way we build it is by proving to ourselves, through our actions, that we are capable. For example, you likely have some level of confidence in your ability to do your job. That confidence comes from showing up every day and doing that job. You've proven to yourself that you can do it. And when was the last time you questioned your ability to walk? I bet you haven't. I bet you don't even think about it. You just stand up and move your legs knowing, at least subconsciously, that you're capable of getting yourself from point A to point B. Where does that confidence come from? It comes from years of repeatedly proving to yourself that your legs will work the way you want them to. After enough repetition, you don't even think about it anymore. You just know.

Terry Fox is a prime example of someone with personal agency. As 1977 began, Fox was a normal eighteen-year-old high school student in Port Coquitlam, British Columbia. Though undersized and largely unskilled, Fox was passionate about basketball. His high school coach had a policy that no one who tried out would be cut from the team, but players had to understand that only the twelve best would get playing time. Showing up early every morning and staying late after school, Fox practised and trained. In grade nine, he got a total of one minute of playing time all season. However, he maintained his commitment to training and practice and, by grade eleven, despite his size, became the starting guard for the team. His dream was coming true.

In November of that year, Fox was in a car accident and injured his knee. Though he wasn't seriously hurt, his knee was slow to recover. In fact, though it was still causing him significant discomfort at Christmas time, it was basketball season and Terry didn't want to miss a game, so he ignored it until the season was over. By March the pain had intensified, so he decided to get checked. It was then that he learned his knee pain was actually the symptom of something far more serious. On March 4th, 1977, at eighteen years old, Terry Fox was diagnosed with osteosarcoma (bone cancer). The recommended course of treatment? Amputate his leg from above the knee. Just like that, Fox's athletic career seemed to be over.

But the seeds of a new goal were being planted. Over the next several months, Fox spent much of his time in the cancer ward where he met other young people, some much younger than him, who were also fighting various forms of cancer. Watching children who should've been at school or playing with their friends instead lying in a cancer ward suffering through chemotherapy touched Fox deeply. He had a great deal of compassion for them, especially as he witnessed cancer take some of their lives. Though he felt compelled to do something, he didn't know what. Fox was just an eighteen-year-old kid. He was a cancer patient himself and had just lost his leg to the disease. What could he possibly do?

In addition to his love of basketball, Fox was a distance runner. Against the odds, he made the JV basketball team at Simon Fraser University in his freshman year. As part of their conditioning, every member of the basketball team also ran cross country. Fox did quite well in their meets, so after enduring the amputation and eighteen months of chemotherapy, he decided he would attempt to run across Canada to raise money for cancer research. He sent a letter to the Canadian Cancer Society stating his intentions to run across the country and raise one dollar for every Canadian, all going to cancer research.

While skeptical of his ability to accomplish such a grand feat, the Canadian Cancer Society agreed to support the run, assuming Fox could find the sponsors he needed. Fox managed to secure partnerships with Ford, who supplied the camper van he would sleep in; Imperial Oil, who supplied the gas; and Adidas, who provided the running shoes. On April 12th, 1980, Fox dipped his toe in the Atlantic Ocean in Port-Aux-Basque, Newfoundland, and began his Marathon of Hope with plans to end back home on the western coast of British Columbia.

Fox averaged a marathon a day on his run. Rarely skipping a day despite injuries, he even ran on his birthday. As the Marathon of Hope gained national attention, money started pouring in. Sadly though, in April, Fox learned his cancer had returned. This time it was in his lungs. He was forced to stop the run in Thunder Bay, Ontario, after running more than 5000 kilometres.

By that point, Fox had managed to raise just over one million dollars. Incredible, yet far from his stated goal of a dollar for every Canadian, which would've been about twenty-three million dollars at that time. A few months later, cancer took Fox's life. However, in the years that followed, others took up his cause. Major donors stepped up, including provincial governments. The Terry Fox Run was created, ultimately spread across the country, and is still held in dozens of cities every fall to this day. As of this writing, the Terry Fox Foundation has raised more than $800 million for cancer research![6] Terry is a national hero in Canada. He is also the epitome of what can happen when someone has a deep sense of personal agency.

How many of us spend our days waiting for someone or something to fix our lives? We blame the government, society, our boss, our parents, and just about anyone we can think of really, besides the person in the mirror. It's so much easier to put the blame for our failures on others, knowing we can't do anything to change them,

---

[6] Tabitha de Bruin, "Terry Fox," The Canadian Encyclopedia, last updated August 5, 2020, https://www.thecanadianencyclopedia.ca/en/article/terry-fox.

than it is to put the blame on ourselves, knowing it means we have to take responsibility for our own actions.

Let me again be clear here that I am not suggesting this is easy or that you don't have legitimate obstacles in your path, some of which are no fault of your own. External circumstances, such as social norms, cultural expectations, and structural inequalities, can limit an individual's ability to make choices and take action. It's important to recognize and challenge these external barriers and work toward creating a more equitable and inclusive society that enables all individuals to exercise their personal agency. Additionally, internal factors, such as low self-esteem, lack of confidence, and negative self-perception, can also hinder personal agency. It's important to address and overcome these internal barriers in order to fully embrace personal agency and take charge of our lives. However, at some point we all have to look at our lives and decide whether we want to use the obstacles we face as justification for why we can't do this or that, or acknowledge our challenges and move forward anyway.

Here's the hard truth: no one is coming to fix your life! There's no knight in shining armour, no superhero, no guru with all the answers. They aren't coming! So if you want to fix your life, you have to do it yourself. There's the saying, "If it's to be, it's up to me," but my version is, "If there's something to do, it's up to you." Go out there and DO IT. Move things around. Take agency. Go out and meet people. Try things. Make mistakes. Screw up. Learn from your mistakes and then try something else. Nothing happens until you take authority over your life.

It's easy to say something like, "If you want things to change, change them." Even though that may be good advice—and it is—without giving you concrete ideas of what you can do and what it looks like to have agency, it's unfair to expect you to follow it. So let's look at a few more examples of how having agency can create massive, positive results.

When working with people as a coach, I often encounter some-one who's struggling to find the motivation to do what they know they need to do. Often the problem isn't trying to figure out what to do, but rather convincing themselves they can actually do it. They'll say things like, "I know I should be getting more exercise, but I just can't seem to find the time." Can you relate? I sure can. I believe it's a universal human experience. There are certainly times when you need more information to make a good decision. You need to read, learn, and better understand the situation in order to make an informed decision and take responsibility. But the far more common scenario is knowing what has to be done and not believing you have the power to do it.

Is it possible at this time in history that people don't know being overweight is bad for their health? Considering the millions of dol-lars put into school curricula, PR campaigns, and health education for people of all ages, not to mention the proliferation of TV shows such as *The Biggest Loser*, is it really possible that a grown adult doesn't understand that weighing 300 lb. is a problem? I don't think so. Information and knowledge are both wonderful things, but they aren't enough on their own to solve our problems. We have to apply that knowledge in order to benefit from it. The problem is, we're often unable to translate knowledge into power.

Every year on January 1, millions of people around the world set New Year's resolutions. January 1 represents a metaphorical new beginning, and many people take advantage of that as a good excuse to make positive changes in their lives. They decide to go on a diet, quit smoking, start exercising, and make many other ambitious plans for how they'll turn their life around.

But we all know the rest of that story, don't we? A study pub-lished in *The American Journal of Clinical Nutrition* found that less than twenty percent of overweight individuals were able to sustain significant weight loss (defined as losing at least ten percent of their body weight and keeping the weight off for at least a year).[7] In other words, eighty percent of people failed to sustain their weight loss. Why? Did they lack self-discipline? Maybe. But I think the bigger issue is that they simply got distracted from their goal and lost their sense of power.

We live in a world of constant distraction. In the few minutes since I sat down to start writing this chapter, my phone has beeped several times and I've been tempted to look at a half-dozen other things, from Facebook to email. It's no wonder we don't get more done; we have so many things vying for our attention. But if we want to reach greater levels of achievement and success, it's imperative that we effectively learn to focus our time and attention on taking control.

So then how do we know what's within our control and what isn't? How do we delineate between the things we need to accept and the things we can and should do something about? To help my clients better determine this difference, I use a tool of the Resilience Roadmap Framework called the Personal Agency Matrix™. The Personal Agency Matrix is a simple tool that quickly shows you where you may be wasting time and energy that would be better spent elsewhere.

The Personal Agency Matrix is based on two psychological concepts: locus of control and attribution theory. Julian Rotter developed the concept of locus of control in 1954, forming part of the social learning framework for understanding personality. It was later refined and added to by other psychologists, including Bernard Weiner. Rotter's locus of control theory goes like this: When

---

[7] Rena R. Wing and Suzanne Phelan, "Long-Term Weight Loss Maintenance," *The American Journal of Clinical Nutrition* 82, no. 1 (July 2005): 222S–225S, https://doi.org/10.1093/ajcn/82.1.222S.

something happens to someone, they'll attribute what happened as either something that was within their control or something that was out of their control. Rotter explains that no one attributes things in a completely binary way, but rather along a continuum so that it may feel more or less within one's control.[8]

THE PERSONAL AGENCY MATRIX™

The Personal Agency Matrix ™

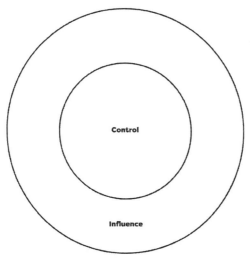

Control

Influence

No control

[8] Julian Rotter, Generalized Expectancies for Internal versus External Control of Reinforcement," *Psychological Monographs* 80, no. 1 (1966): 1–28, https://doi .org/10.1037/h0092976.

Using the Personal Agency Matrix is very simple, but don't let its simplicity cause you to dismiss its impact. Any time you're struggling with stress, anxiety, worry, or frustration, take out this tool and list all the things that are causing those emotions—every single thing you're worried or concerned about, small and large; the things that are keeping you up at night. Once you've listed all those things, ask yourself where each fits on the Personal Agency Matrix. Are the things causing you stress, anxiety, and worry things you can control, things that you influence, or things that you don't control? Place each of the items on your list into the graph in their appropriate spots.

For example, you get sick with the flu. You may consider that to be just bad luck because it's outside of your locus of control. You may think, "Bad things happen sometimes and there's nothing I can do about it." But you may experience this same event and instead determine it was largely your own fault or out of your locus of control. Maybe you think, "I didn't get enough sleep and went to visit a friend who had the flu; I should've known I'd get sick." Someone else may determine that getting sick falls somewhere in the middle.

It has been said that it isn't what happens to you, but rather what you do about what happens to you that matters. While that's true, what is more important is not what you do but rather the meaning you assign to the things that happen to you. When you assign constructive and positive meanings to events in your life, you gain a greater sense of control and increase your personal agency.

Locus of control works in tandem with another psychological theory called "attributional style." Developed by Lyn Yvonne Abramson, Martin E. P. Seligman, and John D. Teasdale, attribution theory is concerned with how and why people make the attributions they do. Why, for example, does one person believe getting the flu is entirely bad luck while the other believes it was mostly their own fault? What makes one person believe they earned and deserve their promotion while another doesn't feel worthy of it and is always waiting for someone to catch them (this is often referred to as imposter syndrome)? When combined, locus of control and attribution theory help explain why taking agency over a situation is so important.

The Personal Agency Matrix™

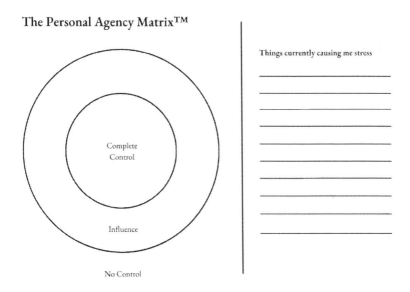

Things currently causing me stress

Using the Personal Agency Matrix is simple but incredibly powerful, and you can use it any time you're feeling anxious or stressed.

- **Step 1**

  Begin by listing on the right-hand side everything that's on your mind. What's currently causing you stress or anxiety? What's keeping you up at night? Take your time and really think about everything that's bothering you right now.

  You should see some results simply by taking this first step. Everyone I know who has done this exercise finds they begin to feel better just by doing the first part of the matrix. When your worries bounce around in your head, you repeat them to yourself over and over and can easily convince yourself that you have far more worries than you actually do. By actually listing them, you begin finding that things aren't so bad.

- **Step 2**

  Once you have all your concerns on paper, place each one in the appropriate part of the matrix. Is this concern something you have total control over, something you have influence over but cannot control entirely, or something you have no control over at all?

- **Step 3**

  Now that you've correctly categorized each of your concerns, begin to address the items in each category more strategically.

  o Everything you put in the "Total Control" category becomes your to-do list. If these things are worrying you and you have total control over them, address them. Take action. Do whatever needs to be done about each item so you can get them off your mind.

  o Everything in the "Influence" category is also something that you can control; however, in this case, you have to do what you can and let go of the outcome. Release your expectations about how things will turn out. Though we rarely have total control over the outcomes in our lives, we *can* control our levels of effort. Put in your effort, and then let go of the results.

  o Finally, the things that you put in the "No Control" category are depleting your time and energy. Every ounce of time and effort you put into these things is wasted. Time and energy are finite resources that once spent are gone. So, we want to spend as little of them as possible on items in this category because they won't have any impact. It's like taking your valuable time and energy and throwing them away. If someone gave you $100, would you turn around and throw them in the trash? Of course not! How much more valuable are your time and energy?

Personal agency is a powerful and transformative force. By cultivating and exercising personal agency, you can take control of your life and shape your future. It's an essential aspect of human experience and development, and one that should be nurtured and valued in ourselves and others. In the next chapter you'll see why you have to temper your sense of agency with the humility to admit that while you control many things, you cannot control everything. The next guidepost is *acceptance*.

 RESILIENCE REMINDERS

- You cannot be resilient unless you believe in the power of your personal agency.
- Whether something is within your control or outside of your control is largely a question of perspective. When you choose to take greater responsibility for the results in your life, you will gain control and become more resilient.
- The meaning you assign to the events in your life greatly influences how you experience

ACCEPTANCE

> *"Acceptance of what has happened is the first step*
> *to overcoming the consequences of any misfortune."*
>
> **—William James**

There once was an old Zen farmer. Every day, the farmer used his horse to help work his fields and keep his farm healthy. But one day, the horse ran away. All the villagers came by and said, "We're so sorry to hear this. This is such bad luck"

But the farmer responded, "Bad luck. Good luck. Who knows?"

The villagers were confused but decided to ignore him. A few weeks went by and then one afternoon, while the farmer was working outside, he looked up and saw his horse running toward him. But the horse was not alone. The horse was returning to him with a whole herd of horses. So now the farmer had ten horses to help work his fields.

All the villagers came by to congratulate the farmer and said, "Wow! This is such good luck!"

But the farmer responded, "Good luck. Bad luck. Who knows?"

A few weeks later, the farmer's son came over to visit and help his father work on the farm. While trying to tame one of the horses, the farmer's son fell and broke his leg. The villagers came by to commiserate and said, "How awful. This is such bad luck."

Just as he did the first time, the farmer responded, "Bad luck. Good luck. Who knows?"

A month later, the farmer's son was still recovering. He wasn't able to walk or do any manual labor to help his father around the farm. A regiment of the army came marching through town conscripting every able-bodied young man to join them. When the regiment came to the farmer's house and saw the young boy's broken leg, they marched past and left him where he lay.

Of course, all the villagers came by and said, "Amazing! This is such good luck. You're so fortunate."

And the farmer said . . .[9]

Have you ever been like one of the many people who spoke to the farmer? Have you judged an event as good or bad before knowing the whole story? Have you ever had something happen in your life that you initially thought was only good, but later realized there were also downsides? Have you ever faced an impossibly bad situation and later realized there were some benefits that came from it?

---

[9] Original Chinese parable written by Laozi in *The Tao Te Ching*, circa 400 BC; Paraphrased from Alan Watts and Al Chung-liang Huang, *Tao: The Watercourse Way* (New York: Pantheon Books, 1975).

I've never met anyone who didn't answer yes to those questions. In general, we can be pretty bad judges of whether something is good or bad, and we often lack the perspective to see the proverbial flip side of the coin. This is one of the many reasons learning how to accept reality more readily is such a worthwhile skill to develop. In this chapter, you'll learn why acceptance matters and, most importantly, how to do it. However, first, it's important to establish our terms of reference. What does "acceptance" mean?

When trying to clarify a term and its use, I've often found it helpful to start by defining what it *isn't* versus what it *is*. For example, if you were trying to explain what a dog was to someone who had never seen one before, you might start by talking about how it's different from another animal they've seen before (e.g., "It's not like a fish because it lives on land. It's not like a bird because it can't fly. It's not like a snake because it has four legs and a tail").

So let's begin by establishing what I'm NOT talking about when I talk about acceptance. I'm not advocating that you should blindly accept all circumstances that come your way as being "meant to be." In the following chapter we'll talk about the next step of the Resilience Roadmap, adaptation, or the ways in which we can change our behaviour and ways of thinking to be more effective in the face of adversity and change. So no, this isn't about blind acceptance or embracing victimhood.

However, it seems to me equally unproductive to live under the delusion that we are truly masters of our own destinies. Countless examples in history and our individual lives illustrate times people have done everything right and things still didn't work out. There are doubtlessly as many examples of times when things worked out despite every reason they shouldn't have.

Whatever your belief system, I think we can agree that some of the things that happen to us that initially seem bad turn out to be quite good. Things that at first appear to be obstacles to our happiness can become the very sources of happiness. The pain of childbirth results in a beautiful newborn. The struggles of starting a business can result in great income and a vehicle to support your family. We've all heard examples of how something bad in someone's life turned out to be a "blessing in disguise." I'm a firm believer in this principle.

The Stoics, philosophers of ancient Greece, called it fate. A core tenet of Stoicism was encapsulated in the phrase "amor fati," which translates to "love of fate." The Stoics believed that while much of life is outside our control (up to fate), we can alleviate a lot of our personal suffering simply by learning to love fate; to love whatever happens. When I first read about amor fati, it immediately made sense to me. Why not try to love whatever happens?

Of course, some events are far easier to love than others. When something happens that we are excited about or were wishing for, it's very easy to love it. It's easy to love getting a promotion, going on vacation, or winning the lottery. But what about when things happen that we deem bad? Are we able to love it when we don't get the promotion, when the flight to our vacation gets cancelled, or when someone we love dies? That's a much different proposition. I hope we can also agree on something else though: just because some of the bad things in life turn into something good, and just because good can be pulled from the wreckage of bad events, it doesn't mean that bad things are actually good or that they were necessary to create good.

While it may be true that 9/11 brought New Yorkers, and all Americans, closer together as they worked to support each other through a terrible time, that does not mean that 9/11 was in any way a good thing. We can't advocate for evil because good can come from it, and the country could've come together through other, more positive and peaceful means. Sadly, human nature being what it is, it often takes a crisis to shake us out of our complacency. In the same sense, the bad things we face in life, work, relationships, or business may cause good things to happen in the end, but that does not make them good in and of themselves.

The more I dug into Stoicism, the more I learned that Stoics were not immune to emotion, nor did the philosophy suggest we should be glad when things don't go as planned. Rather, the philosophy suggests two things: 1) With wisdom and experience, most of us learn that we can sometimes be poor judges of what "good" versus "bad" events actually are and that very few events in our lives are purely one or the other, and 2) Accepting what has happened quickly and without resistance helps us avoid further suffering that comes from fighting against something that can't be changed.

In this sense, then, when I say we must learn to accept the things we can't control, I don't mean that we should passively allow bad things to happen to us or people we care about because some good may eventually come from it. Acceptance, in the Resilience Roadmap Framework, is never about being passive, weak, or lazy. Rather, it provides instruction on how to be more efficient with our thoughts, emotions, and actions so that we can be more resilient in the face of a world where we are often affected by things outside of our control.

One of the most often quoted passages from *Alcoholics Anonymous*, or what is referred to within the organization as "The Big Book," comes from Dr. Paul Ohliger:

> Acceptance is the answer to all my problems today. When I am disturbed, it is because I find some person, place, thing, or situation—some fact of my life—unacceptable to me, and I can find no serenity until I accept that person, place, thing, or situation as being exactly the way it is supposed to be at this moment.

Nothing, absolutely nothing, happens in God's world by mistake. Until I could accept my alcoholism, I could not stay sober; unless I accept my life completely on life's terms, I cannot be happy. I need to concentrate not so much on what needs to be changed in the world as on what needs to be changed in me and in my attitude.[10]

Dr. Ohliger was a prominent writer and speaker in the Alcoholics Anonymous (AA) community until his passing. Reading this passage makes me understand why. The wisdom in that one passage is worth more than many books. Let me stop here to say that I hope you won't allow differences in worldview to prevent you from absorbing the importance of this idea. Whether or not you believe the portion of the quote about nothing happening outside of God's control, we can all agree there are plenty of things that occur in our lives and work that affect us in ways large and small and are completely outside of our control. Unless and until we are able to recognize that reality, we will fail to be as resilient as we could be.

In AA, they use a prayer sometimes known as the AA prayer but more commonly called the Serenity Prayer. The prayer actually predates AA by centuries, but its application in addiction programs puts it in the perfect context for the Resilience Roadmap. The Serenity Prayer begins as follows:

> *God, grant me the serenity to accept the things I cannot change,*
> *the courage to change the things I can,*
> *and the wisdom to know the difference.*

---

[10] Paul Ohliger, "Acceptance Was the Answer," in *Alcoholics Anonymous: The Big Book*, 4th ed. (New York: Alcoholics Anonymous World Services, Inc., 2001), 417.

In three simple lines, we are given the key to accepting any difficult thing we face in our lives. The person who can consistently apply each part of this prayer to every challenge or difficulty they face will be well-equipped to handle whatever comes their way. Let's break it down to analyse why the prayer is so powerful.

God, grant me the serenity to accept the things I cannot change.

How many of us fall into the trap of wasting our most valuable resources trying to change things that cannot be changed? How often have you caught yourself, or someone you spend time with, complaining about the weather? I know I've done it. I've witnessed MANY other people do it too. Maybe it's a condition unique to where I live in Atlantic Canada where the weather fluctuates so frequently, but given what I know about the human condition, I suspect that's not the case.

Complaining is a sure sign that we're failing to accept what we cannot change. Just think about the things we complain about. We complain about our bosses, our kids, our partners, our family. We complain about the costs of food, the economy, the price of gas, and how the government is making our lives more difficult. If you can acknowledge that you complain about any or all of these things, I have one question for you: Has your complaining ever changed any of these situations? I'm going to go out on a limb here and guess that your complaining accomplished only a few things: it made you more tired, it made you more frustrated, and it probably irritated the heck out of the people around you. To find peace and happiness, be more resilient, and cope effectively with the numerous challenges we face every day, we must learn how to accept the things we cannot change.

We have two very finite resources at our disposal every day: time and energy. We get twenty-four hours every day. That's 1,440 minutes.

Given that most of us sleep for six to eight of those hours, we actually have much less time than that. What are you spending it on? If you're spending that time complaining and worrying about things you can't change, you're wasting one of your most valuable resources.

So how are you spending your energy? Are you wasting it away fretting about every little issue that comes up? Or are you channelling it, focusing it, and putting it to the most effective use possible on the things that matter most?

It was April of 2002 when, after waiting on the transplant list for five months, my condition finally deteriorated to the point that I was in danger. I had just completed a Holter monitor test, an evaluation tool in which a person wears an EKG for twenty-four hours so that their heart rhythm can be monitored over an extended period of time. This is often how doctors can detect rhythm abnormalities that occur only sporadically and may go undetected on a traditional EKG. When the results came in from my most recent test, I received the call that my heart was periodically going in and out of ventricular tachycardia. Ventricular tachycardia (VT) is a cardiac arrhythmia caused by the bottom two chambers of the heart spontaneously racing out of control for short periods of time without warning. Short periods of VT are not in and of themselves life-threatening, but they are often a sign that things are going wrong and can be a precursor of a fatal problem: sudden cardiac death. In this case, the diseased heart begins to race out of control and then suddenly, without warning, stops.

My cardiologist called to explain the findings and then asked me to come into the hospital for a couple of days. Soon after, I was told my episodes of VT were continuing to occur. Any of the typical treatments for the condition had either already been attempted or were not options because of some of the other complications with my heart. However, due to the danger posed by VT and the potential for sudden cardiac arrest, it was too dangerous to simply send me back home to continue waiting for a transplant. The only advisable course of action was to admit me to a hospital and monitor my heart twenty hours a day. That way if it stopped, an alarm would trigger an emergency response and the crash cart team would be notified, come in, and use the defibrillator to attempt to reset my heart's rhythm. The bottom line was that I was going to have to live in that hospital until I received a transplant, or until I died, whichever came first.

For the first month in the cardiac ward of Toronto General Hospital, I shared a semi-private room with other patients. I spent most of that time in a state of resentment, bitterness, and anger. Male patients on a cardiac ward typically fall into one of a few categories: they've just had a heart attack and are undergoing cardiac investigation, they've been diagnosed with arterial blockages and are awaiting an angioplasty, or (because this hospital specialized in cardiac arrhythmias) they're there to have a pacemaker or defibrillator installed. In all cases, the typical age of the patients was between fifty-five and seventy-five. Meanwhile, here I was at only twenty-three. It wasn't fair. Most of these men had lived a life. They had gotten married, had kids, and built a career. In several cases, they had found themselves in the cardiac ward because they had neglected their health for years and it had caught up to them. I won't say I felt like they deserved to be there—no one deserves that—but I certainly felt like my life was particularly unfair. *Why me?* was a thought that perpetually ran through my mind.

Thankfully, my cardiologist could tell it was getting to me and made arrangements for me to have my own room. I can still remember walking into that private space. With my mom's help, we moved the few belongings from my temporary, semi-private room into a single room that would be my home for the foreseeable future. As

I stepped through the doorway, the reality of the situation set in; this space, this ten by ten square foot room with four beige walls, a single bed, a nine inch television, and a small bureau, was going to be my home. Whether it would be my home for only a few weeks, a few months, or even a few years, I didn't know. However, given the estimated timelines doctors gave us when I was first listed for transplant, along with the low odds that a suitable donor would be found in time, it was very clear I was likely going to die in that room.

As someone who's often labelled a "motivational speaker" and is thus expected to put a positive spin on everything, I know it would be convenient to write here about how I found the metaphorical silver lining on the cloud and that, despite the gravity and difficulty of my situation, I still took it all in stride. But we just finished a chapter about taking responsibility and being honest with ourselves, so I can't tell you that because it isn't the truth.

Sadly, the truth is that I felt none of those things. The truth is that all I felt was anger, bitterness, and resentment. What had I done to deserve a death sentence at twenty-three years old? Had two dangerous open-heart surgeries as a baby and a lifetime of adversity caused by congenital heart disease not been enough for one short lifetime? Was I not entitled to some of the easy normalcy that everyone else seemed to be living? For weeks I sat in that room and felt sorry for Mark. *Why me? This isn't fair. What did I do to deserve this? When will this end?*

What I didn't realize at the time was that I was operating from a fundamentally flawed premise. At some level, I believed that my life was supposed to be easier. I believed that I was entitled to different circumstances than I was living.

After a few weeks of moaning and self-pity, my mom came to visit me—as she or Dad did every single day—and sat me down for a talk. She looked at me and said something so simple and yet so profound that I clearly remember it decades later. I don't remember the exact words now, but the gist was this:

> Mark, you have a choice to make. You can choose to feel sorry for yourself if you want to. I empathize. You have every right to feel the way you do, but how is that working for you? Where will you be (emotionally and mentally) if you keep thinking how you're thinking? You do what you need to do, but if I were you, I'd start focusing on what's going right instead of what's going wrong, on what you can control rather than on what you can't, and what you still have to be grateful for rather than what you've lost.

Pretty powerful stuff. I wish I could say I immediately recognized the wisdom of her words, snapped out of my funk, and started turning things around. The truth is that my immediate response was dismissive at best. If I remember right, my exact response was, "Whatever, Mom. You don't know what it's like. You don't know how I feel."

I probably deserved a swift kick; in fact, I most certainly did. Mom and Dad had sacrificed so much to support me in every way possible. They were there with me every day and put on a smile and a brave face for me, even though they surely must've been suffering tremendously themselves as they watched their son slowly dying, knowing there was nothing they could do to fix it. Despite all of that, they let me vent and ignored my dismissive, selfish, and rude response, allowing me to figure this one out for myself.

It took about a month as I recall when, seemingly out of nowhere, I had a powerful revelation: I was stuck in that room and there was nothing I could do about that, not if I wanted to survive. If I was going to have a chance to live beyond a few months, I was going to have to wait in that room. There was nothing I could do to make that donor come sooner, or at all. Being angry about that, resisting that, failing to acknowledge that reality, wasn't going to change it.

I won't pretend it was as simple as having a revelation and then being able to instantly accept that situation. It wasn't. Acceptance isn't a decision; it's a process. It's a practice. It's a skill we can improve upon by doing it over and over again. With time and effort, I began to let go. I began to let go of all the parts of that impossible situation so I could focus my time and energy on the things that I *could* control.

> *God, grant me the serenity to accept the things I cannot change,*
> *the courage to change the things I can,*
> *and the wisdom to know the difference.*

How do we accept? It's easy to see the wisdom in the advice that we should accept the things we can't change, but how do we actually do that? It starts with that last phrase, "the wisdom to know the difference." How do we delineate the things we can't control from the things we can?

For weeks I struggled to sleep at night, afraid that I might not wake up in the morning. For weeks, I would start my day by walking to the nurses' station and asking how many times my heart had raced the night before. I would chart the incidents on a calendar. I think on some level I believed that if I kept track of it, I could control it. Of course, I couldn't. In fact, the more obsessed I became with trying to control it, the more anxious I became.

My life changed the day I realized that every time I worried or felt anxious about something I couldn't control, I was wasting my precious and finite resources. I was devoting some of my invaluable time and energy to trying to control the uncontrollable. When I realized that my time and energy were precious and finite, that every time I spent them on things I couldn't change I was wasting those resources, I decided to make a change. I was clearly dying. My time and my energy were in short supply. Suddenly it felt imperative that I not waste an ounce of either one.

I stopped tracking my incidents of VT. I stopped asking how often my heart had raced the night before. I did my best to stop wondering when, or if, a donor would be found. Instead, I focused on trying to be present, on simply trying to be where I was rather than attempting to anticipate what may happen tomorrow or the next day.

This was a process. It wasn't a switch I flipped. I wasn't perfect at this by any stretch of the imagination. I still worried a lot, and I still caught myself wanting to ask the nurses about what my heart had done the night before. I still struggled with trying to control the uncontrollable. But with practice, I got better at letting go. I learned to accept, and in the process regained the time and energy I'd been wasting for months.

So now I invite you to ask yourself these questions: How much of my time and energy am I wasting each day on the things I have no control over? How much of my life am I squandering trying to fix what isn't mine to fix or trying to resist the inevitable? Do I want to keep wasting these resources, or am I going to do my best to leverage them for maximum effect? Will I do everything I can to ensure I spend these finite and precious resources where they will have the greatest impact?

The goal here is to minimize what I call the ONNW Gap™. ONNW stands for "Oh no, now what?" When something happens to us, something difficult and challenging, our natural reaction is to think "oh no!" That's to be expected. It's a totally normal human response when something goes wrong to think, "Oh no, this isn't what I wanted;" "Oh no, this isn't what I expected;" "Oh no, this isn't how I imagined this unfolding." However, at some point later, we usually arrive at the place where we're ready to say, "Now what?" Where we're ready to let go of what might've been, accept what is, and try to do what we can to make it better. The ONNW Gap represents the amount of time and energy spent between those two states. The question is, how big is your gap going to be between your "oh no" and your "now what?"

I bet you can think of examples from the lives of people you know, or even from your own life, in which the ONNW gap was only a few seconds. Maybe you were cut off in traffic and got angry for a second but quickly let it go. Maybe your child did something to annoy you and you reacted in frustration but then quickly forgave them with an understanding smile. However, I suspect you can also think of someone you know who's still living in their gap. Something bad happened to them at some point in their life years ago and they're still angry, bitter, and resentful. They still haven't really accepted it and therefore haven't been able to move forward. Maybe that person is you. Unless and until you are able to accept the things you cannot change, you will never be able to move forward.

Again, closing the ONNW Gap does not mean becoming a doormat or passive victim in your life; it's quite the opposite. We have to learn to get better at accepting what we *can't* control, specifically so we're better equipped to deal with the things we *can*.

 RESILIENCE REMINDERS

- Everything that affects our lives falls into one of three categories: something we control; something we influence; or something we have no control over at all.
- Our energy and time are both infinite resources. To leverage them most effectively, it is critical that we invest them where they will have the greatest impact.
- When you shorten the gap between *oh no* and *now what?* you will have more time and energy to direct at solving the challenges you face.

ADAPTATION

> *"It is not the strongest of the species that survives,*
> *nor the most intelligent.*
> *It is the one that is most adaptable to change."*
>
> **—Charles Darwin**

Congratulations! If you've made it this far, you're not only committed to being more resilient but also actively taking steps to grow your capacity to be more resilient in the face of adversity and change. You've completed three of the seven steps. You're well on your way, but you're also far from done.

Right now you may be thinking, "I'm really not sure if, or how, I can be resilient." That's totally okay. We haven't finished all the guideposts yet. You don't need to know exactly how, you just have to believe that you can find out. Remember, resilience isn't having all the answers; it's believing you have the capacity to find them.

So far we've covered acknowledgement, agency, and acceptance. That's a great start, but we can't stop there, though many people do. Do you know someone who's always complaining about something? One day it's the weather, the next it's their boss, but it's always something. It's as though they have a sixth sense for finding fault with the people and the world around them. They're victims. Someone or something has always done them wrong and they're powerless to fix it. The government is overtaxing them. Their boss demands too much. Their spouse never listens. Their kids are ungrateful. The weather is always too hot, too cold, too dry, or too rainy.

The problem for some of these people is that, in order to admit they have agency, they must face the truth that they've been unable or unwilling to apply that agency to their own lives. It's certainly easier to blame someone else for our disappointments than to blame ourselves. But doing that causes us to *exist* rather than truly *live*, and I don't know about you, but I prefer the latter.

So if we accept that we can't change some things, but we also recognize that we have the agency to change ourselves, what do we do? Those who are truly resilient understand that when circumstances change, *they* have to change. They understand that when the rules of the game are different, they can't play it the same way they did before.

When the coronavirus shut down the world, millions of school-aged children were sent home from school indefinitely. Knowing that infections spread quickly and easily in schools due to the poor personal hygiene of some children, governments in many countries around the world mandated that schools be closed. The ripple effect was massive. According to the U.S. Bureau of Labor Statistics, 62.3 percent of families with children have both parents working outside the home.[11] When COVID-19 struck, those parents had to find ways of providing care for their kids who were home from school all day long. In some cases, parents were told to work from home, forcing them to face the challenge of trying to meet their employer's expectations while helping their children with at-home learning. Teachers, many of whom had little to no technology training, were suddenly asked to instruct students via online conferencing tools such as Microsoft Teams or Zoom.

My wife is an elementary school teacher, and I have a home office I work from when I'm not on the road speaking. We have three school-aged children. At the beginning of the pandemic, Emma was thirteen, Matteo was ten, and our youngest Caleb was five. To give you a glimpse into what our home life looked like at that time, each day my wife would have to log in to her computer once or twice a day to do virtual lessons with her students. In between those lessons she was consulting with her principal and colleagues to learn about the latest government decisions concerning the opening and closing of schools and trying to adapt her teaching methods to suit a virtual environment. Simultaneously, we were both helping our kids log in to their school's networks and Microsoft Teams meetings so they could "attend" their virtual classes. Our two older ones often did two to three hours of virtual class per day, while our youngest had twenty- to thirty-minute sessions a few times a day (I can still see his poor physical education teacher trying to lead a group of kindergarten students through a virtual gym class. It was interesting, to say the least). The pandemic, and the corresponding adaptations made

---

[11] "Employment Characteristics of Families—2021," U.S. Department of Labor: Bureau of Labor Statistics, April 20, 2022, https://www.bls.gov/news.release/pdf/famee.pdf.

to deal with school closures, dramatically changed how teachers taught and students learned. It will be years before we understand the impact that truly had on our kids.

In healthcare the changes were even more dramatic. Emergency rooms and hospital beds were flooded with COVID patients. Many healthcare professionals contracted the virus and had to stay home from work. Others who were only exposed to the virus were also sometimes advised to not come in, for fear of spreading the virus. Healthcare facilities quickly became overrun and understaffed. Those who were still able to work faced impossible demands as they tried to care for more patients with fewer resources, all while wearing gloves, masks, and gowns their entire shift. Non-urgent and preventative procedures and tests were cancelled in order to keep hospitals afloat. As I write this, it has been two and half years since the start of the pandemic and, while the crisis has passed, the effects of the pandemic linger.

I have no doubt that you've been forced to adapt in ways large and small over the last few years, whether you found yourself living the realities just described or not. We've worn masks, used hand sanitizer, adopted virtual meetings, learned new software, and found creative ways to socialize at a distance. The worst of the pandemic appears to be behind us, yet history tells us change won't stop and the next challenge is just around the corner. If you learned anything during the pandemic, I hope it was this: in a world of constant change, adaptation is unavoidable.

In a world where the rate and degree of change is increasing with each passing year, perhaps the most important and valuable skill any of us can possess is adaptability. None of us can predict the future, but one thing is certain: the future will be different from the present. If you're skilled at adapting, you'll have a competitive advantage over everyone who chooses to hang onto the status quo.

Adaptability is a common denominator of people and organizations who remain effective and relevant over decades. A great example of the importance and impact of adaptability can be found in the place where millions of people go every day for their morning dose of caffeine: Starbucks. When the company first opened its doors in Seattle, Washington, in 1971, it was a starkly different business than the Starbucks you and I are familiar with today. In fact, they didn't even sell coffee! Okay, that's not entirely true; they sold coffee, but not in drinkable form. When three professors at the University of San Francisco—English teacher Jerry Baldwin, history teacher Zev Siegl, and writer Gordon Bowker—founded the company, they sold only coffee beans. The only liquid coffee served in the store was for samples. Back then, the company would buy green coffee beans from a local coffee roaster named Alfred Peet, who taught the founders how to roast beans. Starbucks later bought out Peet and expanded to a second location—the one on Pike Place, which is now the name of their signature roast.

In 1982, Howard Shultz joined Starbucks as Director of Retail Operations and Marketing. At that time, Starbucks began selling espresso beans to fine restaurants and coffee houses in the area. The pivotal moment for the company, and in some ways for coffee culture in North America, happened a year later when Shultz went to Milan, Italy, to attend a coffee trade show. The revolutionary changes that were about to take place and change the course of the most successful coffee company in the world didn't happen within the walls of that trade show, however. They happened along the cobblestone streets Shultz walked each day to get from his hotel to the event.

As he took his morning stroll each day, Shultz would stop at one of the many local street-side cafés. While enjoying the great coffee and ambience, Schultz also took notice of the interesting dynamics of the shops and their customers. He noticed how these shops were far more to their customers than a place to pick up their morning caffeine fix. They were social gathering places. They were part of the social fabric of the neighbourhoods they inhabited. People were talking with each other, sharing stories, and chattering about the news. They were places for community.

Shultz also took note of the incredible attention to detail and fine craftsmanship inside these cafés. Everything was done with precision and art. Shultz was inspired. He returned home to Seattle to share his dream with the company's founders. He wanted to turn Starbucks into what he had seen in Milan, but his co-founders were uninspired. They had been to Italy and seen what he was talking about, but they believed it wasn't what Americans wanted. It wouldn't work here. They had a business that was working selling only coffee beans, so there was no need to fix what wasn't broken.

Shultz, though, was dogged. He knew the concept would work, and he convinced the owners to give him three hundredsquare feet in the new location they were opening to serve brewed coffee and espresso. It worked. Starbucks was serving about two hundred customers per day in their first store, but in the new one with the coffee bar they were serving nearly one thousand. It was a hit. Imagine Shultz's dismay when the founders told him they had no interest in continuing the experiment in other stores. They wanted to focus on selling beans, which they thought was the company's key to success.

Shultz eventually left the company to found his own coffee shops, inspired by what he'd seen in Milan. He named them Il Giornale after the Milan newspaper and opened his first locations in 1986. Il Giornale bought their beans from Starbucks and did well.

Soon after, Starbucks began running into financial trouble. Trying to manage their own brand as well as the Peet's brand they'd purchased proved to be too difficult. The owners offered Shultz the opportunity to buy them out at a price of $3.8 million. By 1987, he had raised the money and they completed the deal.

A few years later in 1989, Starbucks had forty-six stores and was roasting over two million pounds of coffee a year. By the time of their IPO in 1992, the company's estimated value was $271 million. Shultz stepped down as CEO for a period but resumed the helm of the company in 2008. As of 2017, Starbucks has twenty-five thousand locations worldwide and is worth more than two thousand times Shultz's purchase price at a market cap of $86.8 billion.[12]

Starbucks is a fantastic success story, but you can only imagine where the company would be today if it had never transitioned from selling coffee beans to selling drinks and all the other supporting products they sell today. The tremendous success of the brand hinged on the decision that Shultz made after visiting Milan. He knew Starbucks had to pivot from selling just beans to selling coffee- and espresso-based drinks. Even after proving the concept, however, his co-founders couldn't see the vision. It wasn't until Shultz was allowed full reign of the company and made the pivot complete that Starbucks truly took off.

As Charles Darwin's work on natural selection illustrates, one of the essential ingredients to survival is the ability to adapt effectively to changing conditions. While we must often adapt on a much shorter timeline than the evolutionary one, the principle still applies:

[12] Zacks, "7 Fun Facts about Starbucks in Honor of Its IPO's 25th Anniversary," NASDAQ, June 26, 2017, www.nasdaq.com/articles/7-fun-facts-about-starbucks-honor-its-ipos-25th-anniversary-2017-06-26.

adapt or die. Those who adjust effectively do well. Those who do not, perish.

Your resilience, then, is tied directly to your adaptability. To thrive in all aspects of your life, you have to become adept at adaptation. The good news is that the ability to adapt is innate. Biologically speaking, human beings are the ultimate adaptation machines. We've been surviving all over the world, in cold and hot climates, through famines and wars, for thousands of years. You innately already have the capacity to adapt within you. When you were born, you were pretty useless. It's okay, I was too. You couldn't communicate. You couldn't feed, clothe, or wash yourself. Left on your own, you would've died within a few days. Slowly though, you learned to walk. You learned to communicate your needs. As you grew older, you learned that certain ways of communicating were more effective than others and certain foods fuelled you better than others. You learned that certain behaviours elicited responses you liked while others elicited responses you disliked, and you altered them accordingly.

You've no doubt had many experiences in your life that have required you to adapt. I know I have. Countless times throughout my life and work, I've been required to adapt to new circumstances. The first significant time I remember well was when I was thirteen.

I grew up in a home with two physical education teachers for parents and three younger brothers. It was a home drenched in testosterone and competitiveness. Everything was turned into a game or a contest, and there was always a winner. I realize that for some people that sounds like a nightmare, but I thrived on it. Very early in life I used competition as a means of motivating myself. My competitive edge allowed me to play sports at a competitive level through my elementary school years. From age six to twelve, I competed at a regional level in three sports: soccer, baseball, and basketball. Yes, basketball. Despite my size, I was not only able to keep up with my peers but also good enough to make the select teams in both soccer and basketball. That is until my heart condition grew worse and I was told I couldn't play sports anymore.

I was crushed. My whole identity as a thirteen-year-old kid was wrapped up in being an athlete. I still had dreams of playing professional sports someday, even though there was no realistic way that was ever going to happen. It took months for me to grieve that loss and accept that I had to find a new passion. But I did. I adapted. I discovered the theatre and got involved in plays and musicals. My skills as a speaker today were planted in those years.

Sometimes, though, even once we realize we're capable of adapting effectively, we still avoid doing so whenever we can. Typically we cling to the status quo as tight as humanly possible, even when we know it would be advantageous to change. It isn't until we're pushed to the point where not changing is more painful than adapting that we finally do something. But what if we could see that adapting isn't as scary as it may sometimes feel and that proactively adapting can prevent pain and provide the results we want?

That is why I developed a tool called The Adversity Archive™. This tool of the Resilience Roadmap will help you develop greater confidence in your ability to adapt effectively to challenge and change. First, you'll mine your life for the proof that you're more than capable of effectively adapting to change. In the second step of the exercise, you'll itemize the times when you have resisted or hesitated to make a change you knew you should make. Finally, you'll be encouraged to proactively adapt in the future by reminding you of the times when making proactive adaptations has had a positive impact on your life or work.

THE
ADVERSITY ARCHIVE™

Step 1: List times in your life (personal or professional) when you've adapted to change.

_____

_____

_____

_____

_____

_____

_____

Were you able to come up with instances when you've made adaptations? Maybe they were successful. Maybe they weren't. We'll look at the results later in this exercise.

Step 2: List times in your life (personal or professional) when you've resisted adapting. Don't forget to note any opportunities you've missed because of your resistance.

_____

_____

_____

_____

_____

_____

_____

Were you able to remember some of the reasons you hesitated to adapt in the past? Maybe you were afraid. Maybe you were uncertain about what to do. Maybe you remember a time you tried to adapt and it went badly. All of that is okay. The idea here is to think about all the things that may prevent you from adapting or at least cause you to delay before taking action.

Now, the final step. Think about all the ways your adaptations have had a positive impact on you or someone you care about. How have you and those around you benefited from the adaptations you've made?

Step 3: List times when making a proactive adaptation created a positive impact.

_____

_____

_____

_____

_____

_____

_____

It's likely easy to think of ways in which the difficulties of your life have been detrimental, but were you able to come up with at least a few examples of ways in which you're better because you adapted? I can think of several examples in my life, though certainly none more significant than the adaptations I made throughout the transplant process.

When I was told I had to stay in my little hospital room until further notice so that my heart could be continuously monitored, I was angry and frustrated. I felt helpless because so much of my circumstance was outside my control. However, while I worked on accepting those aspects of my situation, I began to focus my attention on the things I could change. I wondered whether I could improve my experience by making some strategic adaptations.

For instance, one of the things I've always hated about hospitals is that they give you a hospital gown to wear. We're all familiar with it, right? It's got short sleeves and a long flowing torso, and it ties in the back. For reasons no one has been able to explain to me, it often leaves your back (and sometimes more embarrassing parts of your body) exposed. I hated those gowns. Not only because of the reasons outlined above, but especially because when I put one on and looked in the mirror, I didn't see myself anymore; all I saw was a patient— someone who was sick. Like you, I'm a lot more complex than a single challenge I may be facing. I didn't want what I wore to reinforce the idea that all there was to me was the series of test results in my medical file. So I made a relatively simple adaptation. I stopped wearing a hospital gown and started wearing my own clothes.

You're forgiven if you don't see that decision as an adaptation. After all, wasn't I just doing one thing instead of doing something else? Yes and no. At first glance it sounds like a simple switch, but during the six months I spent in the hospital, I saw dozens, if not hundreds of other patients, and I don't remember seeing any of them make that change. So at some level it was novel and unique, but it goes beyond that.

For the entirety of my time in hospital, I lived attached to a telemetry system; electronic leads that looked like stickers the size of silver dollars were attached to my chest. Those leads connected to wires that then connected to a pack about the size of a portable hard drive. That pack wirelessly transmitted a continuous signal to a computer and monitor in the nurses' station so that if my heart raced dangerously out of control an alarm would immediately alert the nursing team so they could respond. While the hospital gown was ugly and made me uncomfortable, it served a very practical purpose. It was easy to wear that gown while also being attached to those wires. So when I decided I didn't want to wear one, I created a challenge for myself. How could I manage this web of wires? T-shirts were not designed to be worn by someone who's also wearing a telemetry system twenty-four hours a day. However, with a bit of ingenuity and practice, I found a method that allowed the leads to stay on and me to feel comfortable wearing my own clothes.

Ultimately this didn't require a massive change or herculean effort, yet this seemingly small adaptation had a tremendous impact on my experience of that reality. I then began to look for other changes I could make that might have a similar effect. I asked my parents to bring in my sheets, bedspread, and pillows from home. We remade the hospital bed with my linens so that it felt like my bed, and we got a TV and VCR (remember those?). My hospital room had a little nine-inch personal TV, but it only worked with headphones, so it wasn't practical for watching TV with anyone else. We got permission to bring in my own as long as we kept the volume down. I was also fortunate to receive many cards full of messages of support from family members, friends, and even strangers who had heard about my story. Rather than read them and then throw them away, I started taping them to the wall of my hospital room, slowly surrounding myself with messages of positivity and encouragement.

Within weeks, that sterile, institutional hospital room with its four beige walls had been completely transformed. It no longer looked like a hospital room; it looked like a bedroom and felt like home. With my environment now looking completely different, my experience began to change as well. To be clear, the overall circumstances hadn't changed. My heart was still failing. I was still at high risk for sudden cardiac death. My only hope for long-term survival was a one-in-a-million shot that a suitable donor would be found and I'd survive a rare and dangerous triple organ transplant. Yet, even though my circumstance remained unchanged, my experience of that circumstance was transfigured.

It's virtually impossible to put into words just how much my life did transform as we made those adaptations. In many ways nothing had changed, yet somehow everything was different. I no longer felt like I was a patient being held in the hospital waiting for something that wasn't going to happen. I felt like a person who was living my life, albeit unconventionally. I watched movies, read books, and played board games. Friends came to visit. I had my twenty-fourth birthday party, complete with lobster and beer. I was living life. An unconventional life no doubt, but for the first time in a very long time, I felt truly alive again. Remember, we're ultimately not talking about revolutionary changes here—some clothes, some blankets and pillows, and a few decorations on the wall. The changes we made externally took a few hours and less than twenty bucks, but the impact was multitudes of what we invested.

That's what adaptation can do for us. It can allow us to not only make it through tremendously difficult situations but even find ways to thrive in the most challenging of circumstances. It's impossible to foresee every potential challenge or obstacle we may face in our lives. I certainly never anticipated early in my life that I would undergo a heart and double-lung transplant. Our world is changing constantly. What was important yesterday may no longer matter today, and those who are still operating with strategies that were successful last year may soon learn that those strategies don't work anymore. If we're adaptable, however, we can rest assured that we will thrive no matter what comes our way.

Many of us find adapting to change intimidating or even scary, and for good reason. While our evolved prefrontal cortex where we think logically tells us that adaptation is necessary, another part of the brain is fighting us. Our amygdala which lives in the less evolved part of our brain is on constant threat alert. Back when we were living in caves and knew something lurking outside could eat us, the amygdala was an incredibly important part of our brains. Today it's still useful for detecting danger, but unfortunately, it can also create unnecessary anxiety and stress that causes us to avoid making a change that could be beneficial. History is littered with examples of inventions that were initially resisted but eventually adopted by nearly everyone, from bicycles and cars to laptops and smartphones. In every case, those who waited to adapt wasted unnecessary time and opportunity.

To maximize your capacity for resilience, you must work on your flexibility so you can adapt more quickly. Flexibility in this case doesn't refer to the ability to touch your toes or execute a downward dog. It's about the ability to adapt and change quickly in an ever-changing, inconsistent environment. We all have the tendency to prefer our own way to someone else's. We have opinions and emotional attachments to what we think is the best plan and the best way to execute that plan. Whether the context is personal or professional, if we're going to be truly flexible people, we must let go of our personal preferences and objectively consider other options.

Many people are unable, or more likely unwilling, to adapt effectively to change. They're stuck in the old way of doing things and, when their environment changes, try desperately to hang onto the old way of doing things so they don't have to change. Maybe you've worked somewhere where the phrase, "That's always how we've done it" is the common response to any attempt to make improvements. Here's the problem with resisting adaptation: it's always a losing battle. Progress marches on. There will always be changes. There will always be new things. From new technology to new techniques and new best practices, we either learn to adapt, or we die.

Any married person will tell you that one of the keys to a successful marriage is flexibility. As much as you may love your partner, there will be times when you want different things. It may be something as trivial as what to have for dinner or something as critical as how many children to have, but you will disagree. The secret to success isn't to think the same thing and have the same opinion, but to learn how to be open to someone else's opinion and point of view and value them as much as your own.

The same is true in a work environment. You may have a great idea for how to do something at work, but your boss or manager may have a very different idea about how to do the same thing. Who wins? Hopefully whoever has the best idea. Or you could create a brand-new strategy by merging the best of both ideas. Flexibility requires the willingness to compromise and try new things. It's much easier to survive difficulty when you can easily adapt to whatever situation you face. Adapting is not an option; you'll be forced to do it. But if you're flexible, the adaptation process can be far less painful.

So how do we develop flexibility? You can employ what I call the Strategic Discomfort Method™.

THE STRATEGIC DISCOMFORT METHOD™

The Strategic Discomfort Method is the practice of intentionally exposing yourself to new ways of thinking and doing. By practising adaptability in small things when the stakes are low, you prepare yourself for times when you may be forced to make more dramatic adaptations when the stakes are highest.

Some ideas to get you started:

- Let your partner pick the movie instead of you.
- Let your kids pick the restaurant.
- Ask the waiter to suggest what's good and order whatever that is.

Surrendering your will in little situations like this builds your ability to do it when you have no choice. It's easier to submit yourself to chemo treatments if it isn't the first time you've had to do something you didn't want to do simply because it was the right thing to do.

The next time you're faced with a difficult situation, rather than feeling helpless, angry, or confused, realize that this situation is calling for you to employ your flexibility and adapt more readily. The more readily you adapt, the more resilient you'll be.

RESILIENCE REMINDERS

- Adaptation doesn't have to be scary. By reducing our resistance to adaptation we can make it much easier.
- An effective way to reduce your fear of change is by practising small adaptations in situations that have little or no consequence.
- To adapt well requires trying new strategies. Some of those strategies will almost certainly fail. Learn to see this as part of the process.

ASPIRATION

> *ALICE: Mr. Cat, which of these paths shall I take?*
> *CHESHIRE CAT: Well, my dear, where do you want to go?*
> *ALICE: I don't suppose it really matters.*
> *CHESHIRE CAT: Then, my dear, any path will do!*
>
> —**Lewis Caroll**, Alice in Wonderland

The famous speaker and author Zig Ziglar famously wrote, "If you aim at nothing, you will hit it every time."[13] Surely this is what Lewis Carroll was teaching us through the above dialogue from *Alice in Wonderland*. How can we possibly hope to realize our dreams if we aren't even able to define what they are?

---

[13] Tom Ziglar, "If You Aim at Nothing," Ziglar.com, accessed August 23, 2022, https://www.ziglar.com/articles/if-you-aim-at-nothing-2/.

Thriving amidst challenge and change isn't easy. On the road of life there are potholes and detours. As important as it is to define what we want for the sake of giving us direction and realizing our potential, I believe goals, or aspirations as we'll call them in this chapter, are even more critical in fuelling our resilience. In fact, I'll go as far as to say that if we don't have a clear and compelling aspiration for a future that's better than today, our chances of surviving the gauntlet of challenge and change are virtually zero.

The reality is that many people and many organizations that embark on the Resilience Roadmap don't make it to the end. They get stuck right here. After two or three attempts to adapt to their new realities, they give up. Sure, they may recognize the value of adaptability in theory, but adapting takes time. It takes energy. Sometimes it takes a lot of money too. No wonder so many people get to this point and simply give up. They reason that they may never find the right adjustment to make, so they become frustrated and revert to their old ways of doing things. Sadly, once that happens in a world of constant change, their fate is sealed. It won't be long before they become irrelevant, or worse.

If you're still reading this book, if you've stuck it out this long, my guess is that you aren't one of those people who will quit after one or two tries. You're determined and focused. You persevere. You find a way. But can we be real for a minute? We all have a breaking point, don't we? No matter how disciplined and strong we are, at some point we all run out of steam. What then? How are we to keep going even when it's hard, even when it may seem virtually impossible? We must have that clear and compelling vision, or aspiration, of a future that can be better than tomorrow.

Let me stop here before I go deeper into the idea of aspiration so that I can address any potential hesitation you might have about this step. I appreciate that this step may be hard to get your head around.

How are you supposed to be thinking about the future when you're working hard just to cope with the present? When we struggle through the challenging times in our lives, businesses, relationships, health, or anything else, it can be a challenge just to have the energy to keep fighting, never mind worrying about what's going to happen after the struggle is over. Please don't make this mistake. Dedicating time and effort to clarify where you want to go and why you want to go there is often the difference between success and failure.

A properly formed aspiration answers two critically important questions: 1) Where do you want to go? and 2) Why do you want to go there? Let's address each one individually.

WHERE DO YOU WANT TO GO?

I've lived all my life in Atlantic Canada. Where my current home is, I can jump into my car and have my toes in the Atlantic Ocean in less than thirty minutes. When you live this close to the ocean, fishing and boating are woven deeply into your culture. Nautical themes are prominent at various events. The annual lobster festival in my province is a staple of our summer. So while there are no fishers in my family that I'm aware of, the folklore of boating and the sea is deeply embedded in my consciousness. Perhaps that's why the lighthouse and the sea feel like a perfect metaphor for the concept of aspiration.

When fishers go out to fish, they can be at sea for days or even weeks at a time depending on the region and what they're fishing for. Today, most use radar and GPS navigation to ensure they don't get lost and stay safe when a storm is brewing. But in the years before that technology was available, lighthouses filled that role. If you travel through my part of the world, especially into neighbouring Nova Scotia, you'll find dozens of lighthouses along the shoreline. These relatively small tower-like structures are wide at the base and narrow at the top where windows on all sides reveal a bright light that when illuminated can be seen for miles. In the days before sophisticated navigation technology, that light was a beacon for those who worked at sea. It told them where home was. It helped them stay on course when clouds or fog obstructed their view of the shore. It marked the coastline so that they didn't run their boats into the rocks on the shoreline. And it helped them get to their destination no matter how challenging the journey may have been.

A clearly defined aspiration is your metaphorical lighthouse when you're on the sea of challenge and change. Your aspirations give you direction. They help you make decisions. They help you craft the life you want to have.

When you were in grade school you were asked dozens of times, "What do you want to be when you grow up?" Maybe you were quick with your answer, or maybe you were unsure, but the idea that the decisions we make today impact where we end up tomorrow was still planted early in life. You likely selected the subjects you'd take in high school based on what you thought you wanted to do when you got older. If you wanted to be a doctor, you no doubt chose to focus on the sciences, especially biology and chemistry. If you wanted to play in the symphony, you studied music and the arts. Whether or not you find yourself in the same career you aspired to as a young person, you no doubt made decisions at that time that were based on where you thought you wanted to go in the future.

The same holds true for other areas of our lives. If you were someone who always dreamed of having a family, you no doubt prioritized forming strong relationships and trying to find a partner to share your life with. If your desires were instead focused on adventure and discovery, perhaps you chose to prioritize travel. Of course these things are not mutually exclusive, but you get the idea. Our aspirations help us navigate our way through the challenges we face and keep us on the path to where we want to end up.

WHY DO YOU WANT TO GO THERE?

A clearly defined aspiration doesn't only tell us where we want to go, however. It also provides a powerful and ever-present reminder of why we want to go there in the first place. This is especially important when the journey to where we want to go is fraught with obstacles.

I'm a quote collector. From the time I was in middle school, I've always been inspired by wise words, both from the mentors in my life and from those who existed long before I was born. The more I read, the more these powerful ideas have captivated my imagination and inspired me to dream. Maybe you have some favourite quotes as well. One of the most powerful quotes I've ever heard, and one from which I regularly draw wisdom, is from Viktor Frankl's book, *Man's Search for Meaning*. In it, Frankl paraphrases Nietzsche: "He who has a why to live for can bear with almost any how."[14]

If you reflect on your own life and career experiences, I suspect you can think of several examples of the power that a clear and compelling vision can have, even if you've never thought about it in precisely that way before. Have you ever accomplished something difficult? Maybe you graduated from high school or college even though you weren't sure you had the intelligence or work ethic to get through it. Maybe you've built a successful long-term relationship even though you didn't have good role models for how to do that. Maybe you fought through a congenital illness your whole life, as I did, and still found a way to forge your path in the world.

---

[14] Viktor E. Frankl, *Man's Search for Meaning* (Boston: Beacon Press, 2006), 109.

Whatever it is, I'm sure you've accomplished something in your life that you had to work hard for. Something that required you to overcome several obstacles. How did you do it? How were you able to keep going when it got hard? What sustained you in the moments when you felt like giving up?

In my live programs, I typically use the example of parenthood to illustrate this powerful principle. If you're a parent, think back to the first weeks and months of your child's life. Remember waking up at 2:00 a.m. for feedings? Remember the crying? Remember the inconvenient times out shopping or at a restaurant when your child's diaper began emitting a less-than-appetizing odor? What about a few years after that? Remember the tantrums? Remember the never-ending use of the word "no"? How about still getting the occasional 2:00 a.m. wake-up calls? How about the teen years? If your children have reached that age, there's the defiance—the "It's not fair," "You're mean," or "I don't love you" statements—to deal with.

So why do it? Why put yourself through such horrible treatment? Why work your butt off to feed, clothe, shelter, and nurture someone when it takes so much work? There may be a variety of ways that parents would answer that question, but they can ultimately all be summed up this way: their why was bigger than their how. Your why—your love for your child—is so significant that it outweighs the innumerable inconveniences you endure, the sacrifices you make, and the trials you suffer. When your why is strong enough, nothing else matters.

When everything is on the line and you absolutely must find a way to succeed, you find a way, don't you? There's a reason that the expression "if you had a gun to your head" is sometimes employed to challenge someone's thinking about what they're truly capable of doing. By using that phrase, a clear and compelling why—your survival mechanism—is immediately leveraged and pushes you to find solutions. There are countless examples of people who've exhibited superhuman strength in moments of emergency in order to save their own lives or the life of someone they love. The good news is, you can employ this same strategy, even when the stakes aren't as high.

I've been speaking professionally to groups all over the world since 2004 and often take questions from the audience. The most frequently asked question is what ultimately led me to include aspiration as one of the essential guideposts in the Resilience Roadmap: "How were you able to cope with waiting almost a year for your transplant and spending six months in the hospital?" The first time I was asked that question, it caught me off guard. I really had to think about my answer. I gave some obvious answers, such as "I had incredible support." My family and friends all made sacrifices in their schedules to carve out time to visit with me and keep my spirits up throughout that long stay. Had it not been for them, I suspect I may well have lost my mind, or at least fallen into a deep depression. Their support was invaluable.

But there was something else.

It took me a long time to be able to articulate it, but I eventually realized that the other significant factor in my ability to endure the wait, not only physically but also mentally and emotionally, was that at some level I held a belief that things would one day be better. I didn't know for sure that a donor would be found, and I had to learn to accept that my dream of receiving a transplant may never happen. But deep down I could envision a day when I'd be free from the walls of that hospital and able to live a life that had previously been impossible. As I sat in the hospital, weeks turning into months, having the aspiration to one day live a full and active life again became my beacon—a metaphorical light in the distance that I could walk toward in my tunnel of darkness.

Early in my transplant journey, I realized that I'd need a clear and compelling aspiration. I didn't have a name for it at the time, but as I sat in the hospital for days, weeks, and then months, I knew I needed something to keep me going. I began to build a clear and compelling vision of a better future; I began to aspire to something more.

I started imagining what my life might look like after my transplant. I had met dozens of people who had walked this path before me, so I had some real-life evidence of what could happen. Of course, I also had several examples of how things might go wrong. I knew people for whom the transplant never really worked. People who encountered multiple bouts of organ rejection. People who caught any number of dangerous infections. People who never fully recovered from the surgery. While I knew those were all possibilities for me as well, I also knew that allowing those possible negative outcomes to shape my aspiration would doom me to a poor outcome. So instead, I clung to the success stories. I connected with the people for whom the transplant had been a success, and I reasoned that if they could do it, so could I.

Eventually, with practice, I could envision myself living a full and productive life post-transplant. I began to write my first book while still in the hospital, in the hope that one day my story and the lessons I learned along the way might help someone else who had to face the same hard road. I imagined myself as the picture of health, returning to the active lifestyle I had pre-transplant, meeting a partner, getting married, and maybe even having some kids. It was that aspiration that fuelled me day in and day out while I stayed in that tiny hospital room. It was my vision that helped me get out of bed on the days I didn't want to. My aspiration provided the encouragement I needed on the days when a test result showed that my heart had deteriorated even further. My vision allowed me to remain hopeful when so many of my friends from weekly support group meetings got their transplants before I did, even though many of them had been waiting a much shorter time.

Then finally, it happened. On September 6th, 2002, at 10:15 p.m. after another regular day, I was lying on my hospital bed watching TV before sleeping, as I did every night, and my nurse, Gail, came to the door. I thought nothing of it. The nurses would often come check in on me around that time because most of the other patients were long asleep and the cardiac ward was quiet. This was when my nurses and I got to know each other as people. Often these visits led to long conversations about family, friends, and life.

But to my surprise, Gail wasn't there to chat. She came to deliver a message: "You have a call at the nurses' station," she said.

This was a strange occurrence. I had a phone beside my bed in my room. I had lived in that room for nearly six months at that point and had never once had someone call me at the nurses' station. *Who could it be?* I wondered.

Slowly I walked down the hall of the hospital and into the nurses' station. A nurse handed me the phone and I said, "Hello?" The voice on the other end of the line, someone I had never met in my life (and whom I still don't know), responded with a sentence that forever changed my life.

"Mr. Black? I think we have a set of heart and lungs for you."

There was a long, silent pause.

What do you say? How do you respond to something like that? What could I possibly say that would be an appropriate response to learning that after nearly a year on the transplant list, I may finally get my second chance at life?

I spit out the only thing I could muster in that moment: "Thank you."

The voice on the other end of the phone explained that it would be a few hours before the organs would be retrieved and we'd know for sure that the surgery was going to happen. Until a surgeon can physically inspect the organs after they've been removed from the donor, they can't be sure that the organs are suitable for transplant. There was still a possibility that the surgery would be called off. I was told to get ready and wait.

I could hardly contain myself. *What should I do first?* I went back to my room and realized I needed to call my mom. She was staying with me in Toronto, where we had to move to get the transplant, but she had gone home for the night. It was about 10:30 p.m. when I dialled her number.

"Hello?"

"Mom, it's me. I just got the call. You need to come to the hospital. I'm going to have my transplant."

There was a short pause followed by a sentence I was not expecting.

"Are you serious?" Mom asked. Apparently Mom thought this may be a practical joke. Or maybe she was just as dumbfounded as I was that after waiting for something for so long, the day was finally here.

"Yes, Mom, I'm serious. Please come to the hospital."

"I'll be there right away," she said.

While I waited for Mom to arrive, I had a strange revelation: *After the surgery, I won't be able to shower for at least a few days. I should take a shower.*

After my shower, Mom arrived. We hugged, we cried, and we prayed together. An amazing nun named Sister Margaret was called to visit with us. Her peaceful, calm demeanour helped both Mom and me stay calm through the difficult hours before the surgery.

At 5:00 a.m. on September 7th, the surgeons came to get me.

"Okay, time to go," they said very matter-of-factly.

I looked at my mom. She looked at me. We both knew this may be the last time we'd get to speak to each other. I was searching for something appropriate to say.

"I'll see you soon," I said. And they wheeled me away.

That was the last thing I remembered for five days.

I was in surgery for eight hours and in the intensive care unit for the next five days. Most of that time I had little awareness of where I was. Between the strange environment of the ICU and the heavy narcotics I was on for the pain, that time is mostly a blur.

As the days passed and my awareness returned, I realized what had happened. A miracle. I was alive. Someone else's lungs were breathing in my body. For the first time in years, a steady, strong heartbeat was thumping in my chest. I was still here.

The next few months were gruelling. The physical and emotional recovery was intense. As you can imagine, the surgery took a tremendous physical toll on my body. Everything hurt, especially my chest. I've always been very stoic when it comes to physical pain, eschewing pain medication and sedation for procedures for which most patients would be heavily medicated. But I had to accept that being in pain would cause a reduction in my movement and prevent me from doing the exercises, deep breathing, and stretching that were required to begin healing. For months I went to the hospital rehabilitation centre to work on slowly rebuilding my body. But the hardest thing was something I had never considered until I faced it.

For nearly a year I had one focus: stay alive. Everything I did, and most of what my parents did every single day, was focused on that one goal. Keep Mark alive. While that life was limiting, it was also easy in its simplicity. I had no concerns about work, bills, or anything else. My only focus was to do what I could to stay alive. But, once my goal had been reached of receiving my transplant, a giant void was created. The question that crept into my mind, slowly at first and then more intensely, was, *Now what?* After experiencing something so incredibly intense, "normal life" seems almost meaningless. I mean, who cares what we eat for supper tonight? Who cares if you're mad at your spouse? Who cares where we go on vacation? What does any of it matter? I started feeling like everything in life, except the most intense aspects, was meaningless. All the things that give life flavour and joy were seemingly unimportant. It took several weeks of struggling to get out of bed before I realized what I was missing. I needed a new aspiration.

We all need a clear and compelling aspiration. Not just because we want to succeed or be productive but because, at a fundamental psychological level, we need one to survive. When we have no goals, we are rudderless. Our lives lose their meaning. We all need a reason to get up in the morning. When we don't have that, we can't be fully alive. We need a why.

What is *your* aspiration? Do you have one? Is it clear? Is it compelling to you? Maybe you feel like you don't have a clear aspiration right now. If that's the case, don't worry, you're completely normal. I'd like to take you through a simple but powerful exercise to help you find your aim if you don't have one or refine it if you do.

- **Step 1: Dream**
  In this first step, brainstorm. Get out a piece of paper and a pen and just do a brain dump. Think of all the things you'd like to do in your life. What would you like to accomplish? Where would you like to visit? Who would you like to help?

- **Step 2: Ask Why**
  Go through each dream on your list and ask yourself why you want that dream. Sometimes during a brainstorm session,

you think of things you don't really want, things that someone else wants for you, or things you think you're supposed to want. When you ask yourself "why" in response to each of your dreams, if you don't have an answer, it's not really something you want.

- **Step 3: Ask Qualifier Questions**
  Asking qualifier questions will help you distinguish between a wish and a dream that could become a goal:

  1. Is it my dream or someone else's?
  2. Is it consistent with my priorities and values?
  3. Can I mentally and emotionally commit to it?
  4. Can I envision myself achieving it?

  If you can answer "yes" to all these questions, it's time to define your dream and turn it into a goal.

- **Step 4: Define the Dream**
  After you've eliminated the things you don't actually want, you can move to defining the ones that you're truly excited about. If you want any dream to become a reality, you have to make it a goal. The difference between a dream and a goal is that a goal is defined and has a deadline. So define your dream. Ask yourself the following:

  1. What does it look like?
  2. How long will it take?
  3. How will I feel when I achieve it?
  4. What exactly do I want to achieve?
  5. What are the steps I need to take to get me from where I am now to where I want to go?

Let's take a look at how this worked for me after my transplant. I'll set the scene. It was day one post-surgery. I was able to sit up in my bed in the ICU after being heavily sedated but was in and out of consciousness for the first five days. As doctors reduced my sedation and pain medication, I became more alert and aware of where I was and what had happened. I was still alive. Despite the odds, a suitable donor had been found in time. I had to be brought back into the operating room less than twenty hours after the transplant to eliminate blood clots, but overall the surgery was a success and I was stable and on the long road to recovery.

During this time, I'd begun to notice a strange sound that distracted me as I tried to sleep—a strong, steady, rhythmic sort of thumping. It was only as I became more alert and aware that it dawned on me what the sound was. It was my new heartbeat. A strong, rhythmic, steady heartbeat.

For as long as I could remember, my heart had been affected by arrhythmias. Near the end before the transplant, my heart was in constant atrial fibrillation, a condition in which the atria, the two upper chambers of the heart, quiver rather than contract as they should. I was also experiencing increasingly frequent bouts of VT, so the bottom two chambers of my heart would race out of control for short bursts. In other words, my heartbeat was irregularly irregular. It beat whenever it felt like it, with no rhyme or reason.

Since I'd grown so accustomed to this over the years, I didn't notice it most of the time. It was my "normal," which meant that once my heart rhythm was steady and regular it was jarring and reminded me constantly that a stranger's heart was now beating inside my body. I don't really have the words to describe what that feels like or try to comprehend it. I was overwhelmed just at the thought of it. I felt intensely grateful, but also unworthy. I felt overjoyed to be alive, yet also guilty that I got to live while whoever gave me this gift of life was no longer alive. I felt so happy for my family who had sacrificed so much to get me to this moment, but I also felt so heartbroken for another family I didn't know who had lost someone they loved.

Amidst that complexity of emotions, I had a powerful realization. As I felt this strong, rhythmic, steady heartbeat in my chest, I realized that it represented possibility. Suddenly, in the space of less than a week, the possibilities for my life had changed drastically. I began to ask myself the question, *I wonder what's possible now?*

A week earlier, as I sat in the hospital waiting for this transplant, I was in congestive heart failure that severely limited my ability to exert my body at all. I couldn't climb a flight of stairs without getting short of breath. Other than my daily walk around the hospital ward to try to maintain some muscle, I did very little, but I still had to nap every afternoon in order to get through the day. Until the surgery, that was my foreseeable reality. Now, suddenly, there was a world of new possibilities before me.

To be clear, there was still a very long road of rehabilitation ahead. A road filled with risks including rejection of the newly transplanted organs and catching an infection that my weakened immune system wouldn't be able to fight off. The future was far from certain, yet there was possibility. For the first time in a long time, there was room for dreaming again.

Before I was listed for the transplant, my family and I had met with the head of the multi-organ transplant team at the hospital, Dr. Michael Hutchins. I remember he was very kind but direct. We sat down across the desk from him in his office, and he walked us through the transplant process. During that conversation, he talked about the many reasons a donor may not be found for me in time. He spoke about the dangers of the surgery and all the potential complications, including the possibility that even if I made it to the operating room, I may not survive the surgery. Finally, he talked about what to expect after the surgery. Assuming a donor was found in time and I survived the seven- or eight-hour procedure, there would be a long and arduous recovery process full of potential complications. But if I was lucky, I may one day return to work part-time.

I will always remember that last line because it immediately struck me as ridiculous. After hearing this man talk about how incredibly fortunate I'd have to be just to get the transplant, and then how hard the process would be should that happen, the idea that the "prize" waiting for me at the end was to be able to return to work part-time was, shall we say, less than compelling. I remember thinking to myself, *Why would I put myself and my family through all of this just so I can go back to work part-time someday?* It just didn't seem worth it. So I vowed to myself that, should I be fortunate enough to get a transplant, I was going to do everything in my power to ensure that I used that opportunity to the fullest. I wasn't going to settle for survival. I wanted to thrive.

So as I sat in the ICU feeling that strong, rhythmic heartbeat, I wasn't thinking about what was reasonable or logical; I was truly thinking about what might be possible. I used to enjoy running as a kid but hadn't been able to run for years because of my heart problems and the associated shortness of breath. I began thinking about what it would be like to try to run again. Then the idea came: *I wonder if I could run a marathon.*

Keep in mind that when I first thought about this, I was less than a week out from a heart and double-lung transplant surgery. I still had tubes jutting out from both sides of my chest and fluids draining from my abdominal cavity. There were still wire leads embedded in my heart to monitor its rhythm and pressure. I was skinny and frail, weighing less than ninety pounds. I hadn't walked on my own since before the surgery, and I hadn't so much as jogged a few blocks in more than fifteen years. To say that the idea of running a marathon was ambitious would be a gross understatement. It could easily have been labelled as ludicrous, or even dangerous. I was about as far from being capable of running a marathon at that moment as a person can be, and running 42.2 km puts a lot of strain on the body. It's a difficult challenge to meet for the average healthy person, let alone someone with a new heart and two new lungs who's just recently endured a gruelling and traumatic surgery. Yet there it was, this wild idea, and it both captivated and energized me.

The aspiration to run that marathon provided a purpose and passion to fuel me through some of the hardest months of recovery. Between the rigorous physical work that had to be done to regain my strength and the mental and emotional struggles I was dealing with after the trauma I'd been through, I faced a lot of struggles during that time. Aiming at a compelling vision of a better future— that "lighthouse" that was running a marathon—provided the fuel I needed to keep going.

I knew it wouldn't be easy. In fact, I knew it was statistically probable that I wouldn't be able to complete the training, let alone complete a marathon. However, I also knew that the only way to know for sure what I was capable of was to test myself. The only way for any of us to know our true potential is to push ourselves beyond our comfort zones.

Most people don't want to do that. Most of us would rather stop short of our limits because it's safer and more comfortable. It's safer and easier to just decide that something is impossible for us rather than test our theory and see if it's right. Discovering our actual limitations by butting up against them takes courage, hard work, and tolerance for discomfort—things that many of us would prefer to avoid.

To craft a clear and compelling aspiration, thereby accessing the internal drive and motivation that come from it, we need to nurture two qualities: imagination and conviction. Let's break down each one and discuss why you need them and how to nurture them.

IMAGINATION

You may instantly resist the suggestion that you need to use your imagination more often. You may think that mature, serious adults don't live in a world of imagination; that's for kids. You may be tempted to skip these pages thinking they don't apply to you. Please don't do that. In fact, the stronger your inclination to avoid nurturing this quality, the more important it is for you to read this section.

We're all born with an innate ability to use our imaginations. Walk into any kindergarten classroom and you'll see countless examples of kids using their natural inclination to dream and play make-believe. They aren't preoccupied with what's reasonable or logical, they don't care what others may think about their ideas, and they don't self-censor. Whether you remember or not, you were once that way too. Then something happened. Maybe one day at school you shared an idea and a classmate laughed at you. Maybe you worked hard on an art project and someone laughed at it. Maybe you were called upon to read in class but struggled and someone made fun of you.

Everyone experiences the judgement of others in different ways, but we all learn with experience that daring to imagine and dream comes with risk. It can cause people to judge us and ridicule us. As we get older, those judgements may be less overt. Instead of spoken mockery or judgement, our ideas are met with silence or friendly dismissal. But we still experience the same feeling of rejection, and the message is clear: don't imagine or dream because people will make fun of you; grown-ups have to be responsible and reasonable;

the time of dreaming is over. However, I invite you to consider the possibility that it's not only okay for you to use your imagination to dream bigger dreams, but your responsibility to do so.

I'm often reminded that I'm alive today because someone had the imagination to dream of a future that was better than today. The surgery that saved my life hadn't been successfully performed with long-term results until after I was born. There was a time, not that long ago, when the idea of removing an organ from one person and implanting it into someone else in order to save their lives was just a theory—someone's wild idea. If the people with that wild idea had dismissed their imagination as childish or immature, I may not be here today, nor would tens of thousands of others whose lives have been prolonged thanks to organ transplants.

Using your imagination isn't about being out of touch with reality. It's not about abandoning responsibility or pretending you live in a perfect world of lollipops and gumdrops where nothing ever goes wrong. It's about having a vision for a brighter, better future for yourself. It's about hope.

Dr. Martin Luther King Jr. is one of the most celebrated figures in American history, and rightfully so. Born in Atlanta, Georgia, in the middle of the Great Depression of 1929, Dr. King grew up in the racially oppressive South and witnessed first-hand the injustice suffered by African Americans. Like many of us, Dr. King felt the need to do something. He became involved in the civil rights movement, using his voice to speak out against injustice.

While Dr. King gave many speeches and participated in several actions, it was his speech at the Lincoln Memorial during the March on Washington that solidified him as the primary voice of his generation when it came to civil rights. Interestingly, the most memorable part of the speech was not prewritten. It was an impromptu response to being asked to "tell them about the dream."

Here's the famous passage:

And so even though we face the difficulties of today and tomorrow, I still have a dream. It is a dream deeply rooted in the American dream.

I have a dream that one day this nation will rise up and live out the true meaning of its creed: "We hold these truths to be self-evident, that all men are created equal."

I have a dream that one day on the red hills of Georgia, the sons of former slaves and the sons of former slave owners will be able to sit down together at the table of brotherhood.

I have a dream that one day even the state of Mississippi, a state sweltering with the heat of injustice, sweltering with the heat of oppression, will be transformed into an oasis of freedom and justice.

I have a dream that my four little children will one day live in a nation where they will not be judged by the color of their skin but by the content of their character.

I have a dream today!

I have a dream that one day, down in Alabama, with its vicious racists, with its governor having his lips dripping with the words of "interposition" and "nullification"—one day right there in Alabama little black boys and black girls will be able to join hands with little white boys and white girls as sisters and brothers.

I have a dream today!

I have a dream that one day every valley shall be exalted, and every hill and mountain shall be made low, the rough places will be made plain, and the crooked places will be made straight; "and the glory of the Lord shall be revealed and all flesh shall see it together.[15]

---

[15] Martin Luther King Jr., "I Have a Dream," Lincoln Memorial, Washington DC, Transcript, The Avalon Project, Yale Law School: Lillian Goldman Law Library, August 28, 1963, https://avalon.law.yale.edu/20th_century/mlk01.asp.

I've always thought it was very telling that Dr. King didn't talk about *plans* that day. He didn't present a series of slides with his five-point plan outlining his strategic objectives. He didn't bother to explain why this was the logical and reasonable thing to do. No, Dr. King didn't try to appeal to his audience's logic; he appealed to their hearts. He appealed to their imagination. He didn't give the "I Have a *Plan*" speech, he gave the "I Have a *Dream*" speech.

 **THE VISION STRETCH MAXIM™**

There is a simple, yet powerful, tool for helping you employ your imagination and realize more of your potential. I call it The Vision Stretch Maxim™.

The Vision Stretch Maxim™ has three parts: Set, Stretch, Step.

1. **Set:** Set aside fifteen or twenty minutes and brainstorm all of the things you want to accomplish in the next year. When you are done, go through your list and decide which of these is the most important to you. Select up to three that you think you can accomplish.

2. **Stretch:** Take the three goals you just set and ask yourself, how can I stretch myself a little more here? If you wrote that you want to lose ten pounds, for example, maybe you change that to twelve or fifteen pounds.

3. **Step:** Take one step toward your goal with confidence. You may have doubts about whether the new stretch goal is attainable or not. Don't worry about that. Just take one step in the direction of this new goal.

COMMITMENT

Imagination allows us to dream of things that truly inspire us and those around us. And if we dare to believe they're possible, we take the necessary action to make them reality. Which brings us to the second key ingredient required to leverage a clear and compelling aspiration: commitment.

How would it feel if you were as committed to your aspirations as Dr. King was to his? How great would it be if you could find the courage and drive to pursue something in your life with that kind of passion, intensity, and dedication? That's what aspiration does. The world doesn't remember those who were reasonable. The world isn't improved by people who limit themselves to only what's been done before. If you're like me, you can't help but be tremendously inspired by the life of Dr. Martin Luther King Jr. His most famous speech is so compelling that it alone is enough to drive me to try to do my part to make the world a better place. What's more inspiring to me, how-ever, is the lengths he was willing to go to make his dream happen. He wasn't a man of only rhetoric; he was also a man of action. He led protests, organized marches and boycotts, got his hands dirty, and made things happen. Ultimately, he even sacrificed his life for his cause. Imagination is critical, but alone it isn't enough. Dr. King may have influenced a few people by making his speech, but it was his deep conviction to act on his ideas that grew a movement.

So why aren't you living *your* dream? What's stopping you?

Whether I'm working with a coaching client, speaking to an audience member after one of my presentations, or talking with a close friend, I often hear people talk about a dream they have and lament the fact that they haven't done anything about it. I'm always curious to know what's stopping them, and often I'll ask. While I receive many answers to the question, they all boil down to the same thing: there is one thing, and really only one thing, that stops you, me, or anyone else from realizing our potential and living the dream we carry in our hearts—a lack of commitment.

Fear manifests itself in many ways. Some people talk about their past failures and how those weakened their confidence in their abilities. We already know that having a strong sense of self-efficacy is an essential part of resilience, so we know that weakened confidence in our abilities is a problem. We can't allow our past failures to define our future. Just because you failed before does not mean you'll fail again. Many of us are so afraid of failing that we never try a second time. Is it any wonder, then, that we end up thinking of ourselves as failures? We never give ourselves a chance to win.

For others, the fear manifests in ego. We all have a basic need to feel accepted and loved. We need to feel like we're a part of a group. Therefore, we fear the judgement and ridicule of others and try to avoid situations in which someone may mock us or shame us. This is very normal and rational behaviour.

The problem comes when we're so afraid of what others will think or say about us that we allow our perception of their thoughts to affect our actions. For example, it's normal to wonder if Karen thinks my shirt looks nice; it's a problem if I only wear certain shirts because I know they're the ones Karen likes. This need to feel accepted and loved can get so out of control that we become afraid to do anything that may risk the acceptance of others. We may resist doing things we may fail at because we don't want to face the ridicule or judgement of others. When we think this way, we're severely limiting ourselves. Living your life in an attempt to gain the approval of others is a recipe for regret. Firstly, we'll never get everybody's approval all the time, so that's a losing proposition. Secondly, when we live our lives in a way that's inconsistent with our personal values, we end up unhappy. So if you're doing or not doing things because you think it will make someone else like, approve of, or praise you, then you're ensuring your own misery. Instead, focus on what you believe you were born to do and have the courage to pursue it with intense focus no matter the cost.

The last fear I want to address here is one that stumped me for a long time. The fear of success is something that many people have written and spoken about, but for a long time the concept didn't make any sense to me. Why wouldn't someone want to be successful? I can understand being afraid of failure, but why would anyone be afraid to succeed?

It turns out that many of us are afraid of success, or at least we're afraid of what may come with it. We may associate success with dishonesty or cheating. Many of us have grown up with the idea that those who are financially successful have gotten to where they are by cheating or taking advantage of others. Maybe you had parents or grandparents who grew up without many material resources and feel that those who are more affluent must've done something unethical to gain their wealth.

When we achieve success, it can feel very exciting. The problem is that our brain has a hard time distinguishing between the good kind of exciting and the bad kind of exciting we call anxiety. In order to avoid anxiety, our brain wants to keep us on our current course rather than attempt things that will bring success, excitement, and thus anxiety.

Finally, there's the fact that success requires change. Even if you're extremely successful today, to maintain your success you'll have to continually change and adapt to new circumstances. Since we all have a fundamental dislike for change, some of us may avoid success in an attempt to preserve the status quo.

Given all these fears that can stand in the way, what are we to do? Here are a few suggestions:

1. **Connect with Your Why.** We've discussed this in other parts of this book, but it bears repeating here. Knowing *why* you want something is as important as knowing what you want. When you know why you're doing what you're doing, nothing will get in your way. It was knowing his why that pushed Dr. King to continue speaking out and being active in the civil rights movement even when he knew his life was at risk. It's knowing their why that allows an athlete to give up their favourite foods and time with friends in the pursuit of a gold medal. And it's knowing their why that allows a parent to run on three hours of sleep and handle hazardous waste in a diaper out of love for their child. If you don't know your why for your dream, you don't have a real dream yet.

2. **Determine What Will Drive You.** Will you be driven by hunger or by fear? Will you passionately pursue what you want in your life and let that passion drive you, or will you spend your life running away from the things you're afraid of? The choice is that simple. You'll be driven by either pleasure or pain; hunger or fear. Which will it be?

3. **Decide between Comfort and Greatness.** Our Western culture is driven by the pursuit of comfort. Unless you're very poor, you work not to put food on the table (though you may think that you do) but to achieve a certain level of comfort. You buy things because they give you more comfort. You make decisions based on what will give you the greatest level of comfort. There's nothing particularly wrong with being comfortable, but if you want the most out of your life, you have to care about that more than you care about being comfortable. To be in great shape, you must be willing to exercise and eat well, which will cause you some discomfort. Is it worth the exchange? To be wealthy, you have to spend less than you make, pay off debt, and put money

in savings. That will be uncomfortable, but is it worth it? To be a great partner, you must give up some of your self-interest in order to give your partner what they need. That will be uncomfortable, but is it worth it? If you believe those things are worth the sacrifices necessary to achieve them, then you can achieve greatness. If not, learn to get comfortable with being average.

HOW TO BETTER USE YOUR IMAGINATION & COMMIT TO YOUR DREAMS

Below I have outlined a few suggestions for how you can better foster your imagination and commit to your dreams. This is by no means an exhaustive list. There may be one or two things here that speak to you, or you may want to create a list of your own. As long as the things you do help you think bigger and dream more, you're on the right track.

1. **Spend Time with Young Kids.** If you're a parent of children between the ages of three and seven, this one is easy. If not, hang out with a niece or nephew, grandchild, or a friend's child. Kids in this age group are magical because they're still unaffected by the pessimism of the world around them. They live in a world where everything is possible. A world of princesses and superheroes. A world where people can fly and problems are solved with the wave of a wand. While we can't be responsible adults and live in a world of fantasy, we can learn a lot from kids this age:

    a. They're unfailingly optimistic. Young kids are usually smiling and have joie de vivre that most of us have lost.
    b. They laugh a lot. Studies show that young kids laugh and smile far more often than adults do.

c. They're intensely stubborn about their goals. It drives me crazy as a parent when my five-year-old son won't accept a simple "no" to something he wants. But the intensity of his desire and his willingness to fight for it are some things I can learn from.

2. **Regularly Do Things That Scare You.** Some people actually enjoy being scared. It's why horror movies and roller coasters are so popular. But even if you don't particularly enjoy being afraid, you've certainly experienced the joy of relief when a scary thing is over. That rush you feel when you accomplish something you were afraid to do is an awesome feeling. What if you intentionally did things every day to elicit that response? I'm not suggesting you have to jump out of an airplane every day or buy a membership to your local amusement park, but what if you gave yourself small, slightly scary goals to accomplish each day? It might be something as simple as saying hello to a stranger or trying a new kind of cuisine. They may seem like insignificant acts, but over time you'll stretch yourself and become more resilient in the process.

3. **Consume Biographies.** Whether you read them or watch them, consume biographies about the great people of history and how they've done great things by being fanciful. Learn from the great dreamers of our world such as Dr. King, Walt Disney, Mother Teresa, Thomas Edison, Abraham Lincoln, or Steve Jobs. When you immerse yourself in the dreams of others, you become inspired to dream yourself.

Your ability to be resilient is directly connected to your ability to dream. Cultivate your ability to think bigger and create a compelling vision for a better future, and you'll have the fuel you need on the road to greater resilience.

RESILIENCE REMINDERS

- The key to sustained motivation is having a clear and compelling vision of the future.
- Most people underestimate what they are capable of. Practise the Vision Stretch Process and challenge yourself to dream bigger.
- Get clear on why you want what you want. Having a why that matters deeply to you will fuel your efforts until you reach your goal.

ACTION

> *"Finally I was able to see that if I had a contribution
> I wanted to make, I must do it, despite what others said."*
>
> **—Wangari Maathai**

In 2006, a book and subsequent film created a movement that seemed to capture the imagination of the world. For a time, it was as though you couldn't escape it. It was a phenomenon that appeared to be everywhere. It was called simply, *The Secret*.

In case you don't remember it, *The Secret* was a book written by Rhonda Byrne. The premise was simple and very appealing: there's a "secret" to success—a secret that, once you know and apply, could unlock the powers of the universe to achieve and receive anything your mind can imagine. After the book came the movie, in which several supposed personal development gurus of the day appear to tell viewers how easy it is to have anything and everything they want through the power of intention, or what they call "manifestation." If you're unhappy, unfulfilled, or unsuccessful, all you have to do according to these supposed gurus is apply "The Secret" in your life and everything will soon be great.[16]

As momentum around *The Secret* began to build, it seemed everyone was creating "vision boards." Following the recommendations of the book, thousands of people played an adult version of arts and crafts, cutting out photos from magazines that represented things they wanted to own or experience. Hopeful singles cut out photos of handsome men and beautiful women with the belief that this might help them attract their ideal mate. Others opted for photos of sports cars, expansive estates, and luxurious vacation destinations. The book's author and the "experts" who appeared in the film were interviewed on all the popular shows, including THE place to be for selling books at that time, *The Oprah Winfrey Show*.

After months of hearing about it and being asked about it after speeches (and my being always interested in learning), I purchased the book to see what the fuss was about. What magic formula was in this book that had everyone so excited? As I remember it, I bought the book and read it all in one day. I was shocked. Firstly, there just wasn't much to it. I'm not a particularly fast reader, and as I recall it took less than two hours to read the whole thing. After finishing it, I felt like I must've missed something. From what I could glean, the whole book could be summarized into a single statement: if you clearly identify what you want (set an intention) and are open to receiving it, then "the universe" will bring it to you. According to *The Secret*, all we have to do is have the right intention and we can

---

[16] *The Secret*, directed by Drew Heriot (2006; Melbourne: Prime Time Productions, 2006), DVD.

attract whatever we want. Each of us is effectively a magic genie with the power to grant our own wishes.

I finished the book feeling almost angry. Was this a joke, or was this just a giant hoax? Look, I'm all for goal-setting and positive thinking. There's good evidence to support the fact that clearly articulating what you want to achieve and strengthening your belief that you can achieve it increases your chances of success. However, you get nowhere without action. If you stop at intention and don't follow it with action, nothing happens.

Have you ever intended to call a friend and then run out of time in your day or simply forgot to do it? I have . . . more than once. Okay, dozens of times. Calling someone, especially if they're down, can have a significant impact on their day. We all know that. But does intending to call them without actually making the call have the same impact? Of course not! That person has no idea you were even thinking about them. There's a popular saying that "the road to hell is paved with good intentions." I'm not sure any of us are condemned to eternal fire because we didn't follow through on every good intention, but the point is well taken. Simply *intending* to do good is not at all the same as actually *doing* good. Similarly, intending to succeed does not alone create success.

The Secret left out the most critical aspect of goal achievement: taking action on your dreams. You can achieve far more than you give yourself credit for. There are countless examples of people who've gone above and beyond their own perceptions of their limits, but they were only able to do that because they took consistent action.

When I sat in the ICU seven days after my heart and double-lung transplant and decided I wanted to run a marathon, that was a good start. It required imagination, vision, and some courage. But in and of itself, that goal accomplished nothing. If I had set the goal and then sat there and tried to "manifest" running 42.2 km, nothing would've happened. At best, I could've registered for the event, lined up at the start line, and struggled through a few kilometres before getting injured or collapsing from exhaustion because I was asking my body to do something it wasn't trained to do. I knew that if I was actually going to become a marathoner, I was going to have to put in work—and not just a little effort for a few days, but hard work executed consistently over months.

Given my current condition a few days after transplant, going out for a run was not yet a possibility. I had to start small. Every two days for three months I'd go to the hospital gym to do my rehab. Initially, my "workout" consisted of walking for a few minutes on the treadmill and doing some arm and leg curls with very light weights. Week after week, as I put in the work, my strength slowly improved. After a few weeks, I could walk for fifteen or twenty minutes.

My physical therapist warned me that running might not be possible. Receiving a heart–lung transplant is traumatic on the body, especially on the rib cage and thoracic cavity. Often, lung transplant recipients find the impact of running too jarring and painful. I acknowledged my physiotherapist's advice, but once I confirmed that running wouldn't cause any damage or put me at any undue risk, I knew I had to try.

After three months, the last day of my prescribed rehab program arrived. Since that day in the ICU, I had had visions of running, so near the end of that day's treadmill walk I slowly began to increase my speed. My regular walk increased to a brisk one, so I increased the speed some more. I was still walking, but I had to hold onto the treadmill with both hands and pull with my arms to keep up. I increased the speed just a bit more . . . and it happened. I ran. Okay, it wasn't so much a run as a light jog, but it wasn't walking.

It lasted only a few minutes because my physiotherapist was absolutely right; it was jarring and a bit painful. But I didn't care. Jogging those steps for just a few minutes showed me it was possible. The biggest revelation was that, while it was uncomfortable on my rib cage and my legs felt strange having not moved in that way for years, I wasn't out of breath at all. The new heart and lungs I'd been given were working perfectly, and my cardiovascular system handled my increased exertion with relative ease. I certainly didn't yet know for sure whether I'd be able to run a marathon, but I knew it was a possibility. I knew that my heart and lungs would not be what held me back.

Once I had that assurance, I was ready to push harder. After I completed the mandatory rehab program in the hospital, I continued working on my own. I started jogging regularly, first working my way up to a 5K and then to a 10K. Within a year and a half, I signed up to run a half-marathon on May 9th, 2004, my twenty-sixth birthday. A birthday that, a few years earlier, I wasn't even sure I would see.

After training for four months following a strict training schedule, I not only completed the half-marathon but did it in less than my goal time. I was thrilled, but I wanted to keep pushing myself. The goal was a marathon, not a half-marathon. I had to keep going. So I signed up to run the Bluenose International Marathon in Halifax, Nova Scotia, in May of the following year.

I did my best to maintain my fitness for the eight months until it was time to embark on the sixteen-week training program to prepare for the marathon, which started that January.

Permit me to pause for just a second here to remind you that I live in Canada, and we did almost all our training outside. Those four months of training were no joke. I worked five days a week.

During the week I'd do shorter distance runs to work on rhythm, tempo, speed, and strength. After work I'd meet with my training group, and we'd run for between five and ten kilometres, which took between thirty minutes and an hour. Saturday was typically a rest day, but then every Sunday morning we'd set the alarm for 7:00 a.m. and gather together to work on our endurance.

This run was called LSD (no, not acid). LSD stood for long, slow, distance. The idea of this run was to train the body to endure moving for longer and longer periods of time. We went slower so as not to run out of energy (glucose in the muscles) and allow ourselves to go a little further each week. We started our LSD runs by running ten kilometres. We had all run that far many times, so it was no big deal. But before long, we were running sixteen kilometres, then twenty-four. Each week, those of us who had never run a marathon before were running further than we had ever run in our lives. Then we would do it again the next Sunday, and since this was in February and March in Canada, there were days when the challenge wasn't just the distance. Some days it was incredibly cold. Other days the road was slippery from ice. Some days it was snowing, or the wind was blowing so hard you could hardly see. But we just kept going.

Finally, race weekend arrived. All week, the forecast for race day had been getting increasingly dire. Undeterred, I drove the three hours from my home to Halifax to run the following morning. My wife, who had been training with her friend for the half-marathon, came with me. We would all start together, and then she and her friend would be there to cheer me on after they finished.

The night before the race, I set my alarm just in case. I never sleep well the night before a big event. There are too many nerves. When you've dedicated four months of focused work to achieving something you've never done, nerves are only natural. Sure enough, I tossed and turned most of the night. After waking up in the morning before the alarm, I walked over to the large window in our hotel room and pulled back the curtains to check the weather. It was raining—sideways. Immediately I turned on the TV and tuned in to the weather station. I'll never forget the words of the meteorologist: "Well it isn't technically a hurricane." *Oh good*, I thought sarcastically. The weatherman continued, "However, the forecast is for periods of heavy rainfall, and winds are expected to gust 120–140 kilometres per hour."

This would be a great time to tell you how I was faced with this tremendous challenge and immediately stepped up to meet it. Wouldn't it be great if I told you that I looked out the window, saw the sheets of rain, heard the gusting wind, and proclaimed, "What a great challenge. Let's go run!"?

That would definitely be a great story, but it isn't the story I can tell you because that isn't what happened. I didn't look at the challenge and embrace it. In fact, when I saw that storm, the only running I wanted to do was to run away from the challenge. It took the prodding and encouragement of my wife to even get me out the door and start the race.

The start time was pushed back for hours as race organizers scrambled to cope with the disruption caused by the storm. The winds had blown over water stations and mile markers. In fact, they were gusting so much that it was deemed unsafe for us runners to cross a bridge that was on the route, so the organizers were forced to change the entire course at the last minute.

Finally, though, we got started. I still remember running out the door of the arena where we'd been sheltering from the storm during the long delay. After a few hours of enjoying some snacks and music, the time had come to run. A large door opened, and hundreds of runners gathered at the exit. The starter's pistol went off and we charged out the door—out of the dry safety of the arena and into the pouring rain and gusting wind.

The first few kilometres were hard. It was challenging to get used to the wind pushing against me slowing me down and the rain pelting my face making it hard to see. Thankfully I was running alongside a marathon veteran. She had been one of my guides through the long months of training, and she encouraged me to keep going even when I wasn't sure if that was what I wanted to do.

Whenever you're in the midst of a difficult situation, it's easy to become disoriented. It's hard to know which way to go and what to do. It may seem like the logical conclusion is to not do anything. It may seem like weighing your options and waiting for more evidence to come in is the prudent choice. I won't go as far as to say that there's never a time when it makes sense to wait for more information or give yourself more time to prepare, but in my experience working with coaching clients, most people tend to err on the side of waiting too long rather than acting too soon.

This is another part of the Resilience Roadmap where so many people get stuck. Realistically, they know what they should do, but they hesitate. They want to be sure. They want some way to guarantee their action will create the result they want. They want some assurance they aren't making a mistake. And they want to be sure they've planned for every eventuality or wait until the conditions improve before they do anything. The reality, however, is that the conditions will never be perfect, and we can never plan for every eventuality because we can't predict the future. If we wait for those things to happen before we act, we'll never do anything. We'll never have everything all figured out; in fact, if you ever think you do, you should be worried. Those who succeed don't wait for the right time, they make the time right. They just take action. They just do something, even if they have no idea whether it will work. Even if we're quite sure it won't work, trying something and failing will still bring us closer to our goals than doing nothing at all, assuming of course that we learn something from our failures. If you want to achieve anything of significance in your life, you have to take action—decisive, focused action—and then commit to yourself that you won't quit until you reach your goal.

You've heard the story dozens of times before:

The tortoise and the hare decide to have a race. The hare is supremely confident, and why not? He knows he's much faster than the tortoise. His genetics and skills make him the obvious favourite in a race. What chance does a slow and plodding tortoise have in a test of speed against him?

As the race begins, things go exactly as expected. The hare, who's known to be faster, quickly gets a big lead. Before long he's so far ahead he can't even see the tortoise. Sure of his victory, the hare sees no reason to push himself needlessly. He decides to take a break and rest. After all, the tortoise is so far back and moving so slowly, if he hasn't quit already it will be hours before he catches up.

The hare lays down under a tree to rest. He's so comfortable, he falls asleep. Eventually, the tortoise, who has continued to slowly plod along, comes upon the hare, who is sorely unaware that hours have passed and is still fast asleep. The tortoise continues slowly but steadily on his way.

Finally, hours after the tortoise passes by, the hare awakens to discover that his short rest was actually a deep sleep. The tortoise has passed him, and he's now losing the race. He takes off at top speed trying to make up for lost time.

After running all-out for some time, the hare can finally see the tortoise in the distance. It's only a matter of time before he catches up. There's just one problem: the finish line is close; so close, in fact, that the slow and plodding tortoise is able to reach the line first and win the race.[17]

The Tortoise and the Hare, the most famous of Aesop's Fables, is the simplest illustration of the powerful impact perseverance can have on our results, and perseverance is an essential part of resilience. The tortoise won the race because he never stopped moving forward. Despite the odds against him, and despite being severely outmatched by the speed of the hare, he was unrelenting. He plodded forward step after step. There was no way to know that the hare would take that break. Given the available information, the logical conclusion was that the tortoise would lose and lose badly, but that didn't dissuade him. He persevered despite all the odds and attained victory.

It's important to not oversimplify this lesson, however. The perseverance of the tortoise wouldn't have been enough on its own. If the hare had simply run the race to the best of his ability, he would've easily won no matter the effort of the tortoise. Perseverance alone isn't enough. What I've found, though, and perhaps you can relate to this, is that those who persevere tend to eventually find windows of opportunity. If you give yourself enough chances to succeed, eventually you will.

The *Tortoise and the Hare* model of resilience is simple: if you never quit, you never fail. How often are we defeated as soon as we encounter resistance? How quickly are we willing to give up on our goals and dreams when things become difficult? We live in a very image-conscious world. We share filtered images on Instagram

---

[17] Paraphrased from Jerry Pinkney and Aesop, *The Tortoise & the Hare* (New York, NY: Boston, Little, Brown and Company, 2013).

and idealized versions of our lives on Facebook. People are becoming famous, wealthy, and "successful" seemingly without effort or obstacle. Reality shows such as *American Idol, Million Dollar Listing,* and *America's Next Top Model* promote the perception that success happens quickly and easily. Go to an audition and get a few votes, and you can become a superstar. Follow the brash style of the Realtors on *Million Dollar Listing,* and you can become a real-estate mogul. If you're born with good genes and a flair for fashion, you can be America's next top model.

Intellectually, we realize that shows like these don't tell the whole story. They sell themselves by appealing to the impatience and insecurity in all of us. By portraying significant achievements as not only attainable but easily accomplished, they hook us. It's a convenient idea to believe that you and I are just a few smart real-estate deals away from becoming the next real-estate mogul of New York. It would be wonderful to think that I'm just a step away from my own record deal, and all I need is the chance to be "discovered."

The problem with this thinking is that it's a recipe for disaster. It creates big dreams built on foundations of sand. As soon as the first wave of opposition rolls in, the sand is washed away and the dream crumbles. When you believe that success can and should come quickly and easily, your reaction to opposition and obstacles is naturally to feel deflated and defeated. How many of those who audition for *American Idol* and get turned away ever go back to audition again? Some, but not many. How many, after being rejected by Simon, give up on not only their musical dreams but all their dreams? Probably more than we know.

That's why having fortitude is such a critical component of being resilient and why I've saved it to the end to talk about it. Statistically, you're more likely to remember the last thing you read than the beginning or middle. Being that fortitude is such an essential element of resilience, I wanted to do everything I could to ensure that the concept sticks with you.

Fortitude is not exactly a word most of us use every day, so perhaps a definition would be useful. According to the *Oxford Learner's Dictionary*, fortitude means "courage shown by somebody who is suffering great pain or facing great difficulties."[18] I've always believed that we can only truly fail if we fail to persist. If we give something our very best effort and refuse to quit no matter what comes our way, it's hard to argue that we failed. We may not have reached the success we wanted, but we didn't fail; we just learned a lesson.

Thomas Edison, the most prolific inventor of all time, is a good example of fortitude. He has a record 1,193 US patents registered in his name, including the microphone, the movie camera, and the phonograph. The invention for which he is best known, however, is the lightbulb. Interestingly, Edison didn't actually invent the lightbulb. There were several versions of the lightbulb already in existence in Edison's time, but Edison created the filament that allows lightbulbs to burn for much longer periods of time.

When Edison was working on his version of the lightbulb and his filament, he had to run many experiments. Edison's legacy includes the story of his response to a reporter's question about how he persevered through thousands of failed experiments. Edison quipped, "I didn't fail 10,000 times. I found 10,000 ways that didn't work."[19] No one really knows how many experiments Edison ran on that lightbulb. What we do know is that he worked on it for years,

---

[18] *Oxford Learner's Dictionary*, s.v. "fortitude," accessed August 27, 2022, https://www.oxfordlearnersdictionaries.com/us/definition/english/fortitude?q=fortitude.

[19] Erica R. Hendry, "7 Epic Fails Brought to You by the Genius Mind of Thomas Edison," *Smithsonian Magazine*, November 20, 2013, https://www.smithsonianmag.com/innovation/7-epic-fails-brought-to-you-by-the-genius-mind-of-thomas-edison-180947786/.

and we know from his quote that he was very solution oriented. Edison didn't see the problems; he saw every failure as an opportunity to learn and get a step closer to finding the solution.

How hard and for how long are you willing to work for what you want? Will you give it one try? Three? Or will you do whatever it takes for as long as it takes until you get the result you want? Those who are resilient don't allow quitting to be an option. They know that while things may get tough, and while there will be difficult times on the journey, those who succeed are those who persist. They have fortitude.

When I speak to audiences around the world to talk about resilience, I specifically talk about having fortitude. I'll ask them whether they think of themselves as a determined, persistent person. In speaking with and coaching thousands of people, I've learned that most of us don't give ourselves the credit we deserve. Most of us believe we're weak. We discount our abilities and carry a tremendous amount of self-doubt.

Contrary to what you may believe about yourself, however, plenty of research shows that most people have a great capacity for resilience and persistence. While many people seem to be innately persistent, they appear that way only because they've learned the skill over time, whether on purpose or by accident.

One of the great challenges we face as a society today is our tendency toward convenience and comfort. While there's nothing wrong with either of these things per se, when we place too much importance on them, we risk losing the benefits and lessons learned through struggle and failure. Over the last two decades we've become a society that overprotects our children. The phenomenon of "helicopter parents" who hover over their children in an attempt to ensure they never fall or fail is sowing dangerous seeds. We are raising a generation of children who've never experienced failure or disappointment. They don't understand what it feels like to not get what they want, and they haven't had to work hard for much of anything.

While I'm not advocating that we should leave our children to fend for themselves, there is value in allowing children to fail. Great learning takes place when someone is allowed to experience the cause-and-consequence relationship of their actions. When we shelter kids from these experiences, we in effect rob them of the tools they need to develop fortitude. Fortitude is like a muscle; it's there in all of us, but in order for it to grow strong and be useful, it needs to be exercised.

Consider, for example, a little girl who's learning to ride her bike. As with any child, her first attempts are clumsy. She's intimidated and doesn't want to fall. She'll start out pedalling once or twice and then tip over. She gets back up and tries again. This time she pedals four or five times before she falls. The third time, when she starts to tip, she shifts her weight, corrects her direction, and stays up. After a few more tries she's riding with confidence.

Now, what happens if that same child is learning to ride her bike, but her father decides to put training wheels on it? As soon as the little girl gets on the bike it's stable and easy to balance. She has immediate success and can pedal freely. It would seem like this is a great solution to a problem. A normal bike tips over, so we put training wheels on the bike and now it doesn't tip. Perfect! There's just one problem. Because the bike never tips, the girl never has to shift her weight to regain her balance. She hasn't actually learned all the skills necessary to ride a bike well. She's learning to steer and pedal, but she hasn't learned how to balance. As long as the training wheels stay on, she's fine. Take them off, and she won't be able to ride the bike.

That's what we do when we don't allow people to experience failure and resistance. When we're no longer experiencing struggle, we're no longer forced to adjust, accommodate, and innovate. We lose our ability to persist because we've learned that success is supposed to come easily and quickly. When it doesn't, we get frustrated and angry. It's what Martin Seligman, a psychologist at the University of Pennsylvania, and his colleagues termed, "learned helplessness."

Seligman, along with his associates Peterson and Maier, conducted a study in which dogs and rats that were raised in the laboratory and confined to a box were given uncontrollable shock. After a while, they would stop trying to escape the box and passively accept the shock. Later, when the box was removed or they were given an opportunity to escape, they didn't even try.[20] This, "learned helplessness" is a psychological phenomenon in which an individual becomes passive and unable to take action in response to a negative or aversive situation, even if they have the ability to change it. This occurs when an individual experiences repeated failures or failures that seem beyond their control, leading them to believe that they have no power to influence the outcome of events.

Sometimes though, the issue isn't that we believe the problem isn't fixable but that we're missing the persistence required to do it. Abram Amsel and Paul Wong, psychologists at the University of Toronto, developed something called "frustration theory." The frustration effect is a related concept that refers to the negative emotional and cognitive responses that can occur when an individual is unable to achieve a desired goal or outcome due to external barriers or constraints. Frustration can lead to feelings of anger, disappointment, and anxiety, and it can also lead to learned helplessness

[20] Martin E. Seligman and Steven F. Maier, "Failure to Escape Traumatic Shock," *Journal of Experimental Psychology* 74, no. 1 (1967): 1–9, https://doi.org/10.1037/h0024514.

if an individual becomes overwhelmed by the inability to achieve their goals.

Amsel and Wong discovered that if someone experiences several instances of action followed by a reward, then completes an action and receives no reward, they experience frustration, or a phenomenon they termed the "frustration effect."[21] Contrastingly, the researchers noted that those who experienced a mix of reward and no reward developed greater persistence and increased their efforts to achieve the reward the next time. In fact, they noted that animals exposed to a variety of uncontrollable events slowly over time, such as shock, non-reward, and aversive stimulation, were able to adapt and showed more courage in the face of similar obstacles the next time around. The animals learned optimism and persistence, and they demonstrated that in a similar but different situation the next time. In other words, they learned fortitude. If rats and dogs can do it, so can we.

I've completed four marathons. When people learn that I've run 42.2 km four different times and that I've done so with two transplanted lungs and a transplanted heart, they're amazed and often say things like, "I could never do that" or "I wish I could run a marathon, but I can barely run two miles." While I appreciate the sentiment, I often have to hold back from challenging the assumptions of these people. What makes them think that there's something special about me that allows me to run a marathon and not them? Physiologically, I have several disadvantages that could logically be used as reasons why I shouldn't be able to run a marathon, the obvious one being that I'm using someone else's lungs and heart to do it.

---

[21] James J. Hug, "Frustration Effects after Varied Numbers of Partial and Continuous Reinforcements: Incentive Differences as a Function of Reinforcement Percentage," *Psychonomic Science* 21, (1970): 57–59, https://doi.org/10.3758/BF03332433.

As of this writing, I am the only man to have run a marathon after receiving a heart and double-lung transplant. Besides that obstacle though, I'm short and stocky. In fact, I'm very short, just 4'11", and I weigh about 125 lb. That's a fair bit of weight to carry on very short strides. Compare that to the physiology of Meb Keflezighi, the Eritrean-born American runner who has won the New York and Boston Marathons and the silver medal at the 2012 Olympics. Keflezighi has a more typical marathoner's physique. He also weighs 125 lb. but is six inches taller than me.

Here's the thing about running a marathon that most people who've never done it don't understand: virtually anyone can do a marathon; most people just don't want to. I say that partially tongue-in-cheek, but I believe it to be an accurate statement. The thing that's special about the marathon is that it's an endurance sport in the purest form. You don't need a great deal of skill or knowledge to do it. You don't need a particular physique or specialized equipment. You only need some training and a fierce desire to finish. A marathon is a gruelling, punishing event. The event is demanding, but the training to prepare properly is perhaps even tougher. Typically, someone new to the sport will take six months to a year to get ready. It involves early mornings and long, often lonely runs. There's hill training and shorter running to develop speed and strength, cross-training and stretching to maintain flexibility and prevent injury, and long endurance runs to prepare the body for the punishing pounding of 42.2 km of feet on pavement.

Maybe what makes the marathon most special is that it poses the same level of difficulty for everyone who does it. A marathon may have a few hundred runners, or tens of thousands. Its participants may range in speed and ability from the elite sub 2:30:00 marathoner to those who take over six hours to finish. Events are held all over the world, and participants range from teens to people in their eighties. But despite all the differences, at any given event on any weekend anywhere in the world, every runner has to cover the same 42.2 km course and deal with the same challenges. The elite runner can suffer the same pain, the same injuries, and the same fatigue as the weekend warrior. Granted, they'll do it much more quickly, but the symptoms and experience can be comparable. The elation of crossing the finish line is comparable whether the clock reads 2:29 or 5:59. The victory is finishing, and if you believe you can do it and make a real commitment to reach the finish line, you're already halfway there.

If we want to reach greater levels of achievement and success in our lives, it's imperative that we effectively learn to focus, be patient, and persevere.

FOCUS

What does focus have to do with resilience? Everything. In times of adversity, our resources are particularly strained. If you've ever had a time when you were particularly stressed or going through something particularly difficult, you know it can be very draining. Energy is at a premium. During times like this it becomes increasingly important to get the very most we can from our time and energy, and the key to this is focus. But there's a problem: most of us are chronically, compulsively distracted. I may not even have to tell you the biggest cause and culprit of our distraction; you likely have it in your pocket right now, or maybe you're even holding it in your hand. It's your phone.

When we're less productive, we're less effective as a result. A study conducted by Bill Thornton, a professor of psychology at the University of Southern Maine, challenged two groups of students to complete cognitively demanding tasks. The first group was to complete the tasks with a cell phone placed close by. The second group was to complete the same tasks with a small cell phone-sized notebook placed in the same spot. The group that could see the cell phone performed measurably worse than those who saw only the notebook.[22] Merely being in the presence of a phone makes us less effective and, essentially, dumber. Imagine the impact when we're actually *using* that phone.

Lack of focus has serious consequences. In a new study published in the *Journal of Experimental Psychology: Human Perception and Performance*, researchers found that experiment subjects who performed a task that required intense focus performed poorly when they received a text or call notification on their phone during the experiment. When the notifications broke their concentration, the subjects had more incorrect answers and were more likely to make rapid guesses. Subjects who received notification of a call, even if they didn't pick it up, were three times likelier to make mistakes. The researchers had subjects who didn't know the point of the experiment use their own phones, which they say made it more likely that a notification would be distracting since the subjects were expecting those interruptions to be personally relevant.[23]

The reason for these results is that, in spite of all the multitasking we do, our brains aren't really that good at it. An article published in *The Telegraph* in the UK reported that chatty colleagues, mobile phone notifications, and the view out of the window lead to the

---

[22] Bill Thornton et al., "The Mere Presence of a Cell Phone May Be Distracting: Implications for Attention and Task Performance," *Social Psychology* 45, no. 6 (2014): 479–488, https://doi.org/10.1027/1864-9335/a000216.

[23] Cary Stothart, Ainsley Mitchum, and Courtney Yehnert, "The Attentional Cost of Receiving a Cell Phone Notification," *Journal of Experimental Psychology: Human Perception and Performance* 41, no. 4 (2015): 893–897, https://doi.org/10.1037/xhp0000100.

average worker wasting sixty hours every month.[24] Assuming even a minimum wage salary of $11/hr., that costs the average company $660/employee/month! If you had ten employees, those distractions would cost you $792,000 a year!

An average person is capable of a certain amount of productivity each day. Just think of your average daily schedule. In one day, you might exercise for forty-five minutes, do six hours of office work, drive several miles, eat multiple times, hold two meetings, and write two dozen emails, all while your brain is completing dozens of subconscious tasks and calculations you aren't even aware of. We are capable of a tremendous amount of productive output. There's just one problem: our capacity for work is significantly impeded by our lack of focus.

A study at the University of California Irvine led by Gloria Mark found that it takes people an average of twenty-three minutes to get back on track after switching from one task to another.[25] So every time you take a "break" to check an email, go to the bathroom, grab a coffee, or have a smoke, you aren't just losing the time you're on break, you're also losing an extra twenty to thirty minutes slowly getting yourself back into the task at hand.

So what are we to do? Is this just the new reality of living in a technologically advanced world? Are we doomed to a life of checking Facebook and email every fifteen minutes? Not necessarily. If you're someone who struggles to stay focused, here are some things

---

[24] Susanna Huth, "Employees Waste 759 Hours Each Year Due to Workplace Distractions," *The Telegraph*, June 22, 2015, https://www.telegraph.co.uk/finance/jobs/11691728/Employees-waste-759-hours-each-year-due-to-workplace-distractions.html.

[25] Jennifer Robison, "Too Many Interruptions at Work?" *Gallup Business Journal*, June 8, 2006, https://news.gallup.com/businessjournal/23146/too-many-interruptions-work.aspx.

you can do to help yourself get back on track as well as prevent yourself from becoming distracted in the first place:

- **Block Time.** This time-management technique has transformed the way I do work. As an entrepreneur, I have the blessing and the curse of having almost complete autonomy over my schedule. I can do what I want to do when I want to do it. That sounds ideal, until you realize it means that if I don't feel like doing my work today, I don't have to. If I want to watch three episodes of my new favourite show on Netflix, I can. Of course, there are consequences to this. The way I prevent myself from falling into this trap is by blocking out my time. I created a schedule in which I break things up into ninetyto one hundred and twentyminute blocks of time and assign a particular task or project to each one. For example, to write this book, I set aside two-hour writing windows when all I did was write.
- **Create Space.** We need mental and physical space to create and do our best work, and most of us never give ourselves the space we need. Yet we wonder why we aren't more productive. Warren Buffett has been quoted in several publications saying that he blocks out chunks of time in his day just to sit and think. He's found that having this "free time" allows him the mental space to do some of his best work.[26]
- **Shut Out Distractions.** We've already talked about how easy it is to become distracted by the multitude of beeps, rings, and pings we receive from our phones. Add to this the various interruptions from people who need things from us, and it's no wonder we have a hard time getting anything done. You can change

---

[26] Chris Winfield, "This Is Warren Buffett's Best Investment Advice," *Time*, July 23, 2015, https://time.com/3968806/warren-buffett-investment-advice/.

a lot of this simply by being intentional about how you interact with technology and people. Shut off your email program after you check your mail (or at least turn off notifications). Close your office door and hang a "Do Not Disturb" sign on it. Close your internet browser except when you're actively doing something that requires its use. Turn off your cell phone during blocks of important work time. By doing just a few of these simple things, you can dramatically increase your focus and productivity.

- **Take Naps.** Despite our best efforts, most of us aren't getting enough sleep. Fatigue and sleepiness impact our ability to focus. But there is hope. Research done at the University of Harvard showed that carving out as little as twenty minutes to take a nap can improve memory and problem-solving ability.[27]

Resilience is an art and a science. It requires you to master many skills and attitudes and be continuously adapting to an ever-changing environment. Those who do it best are always learning. Learning may seem like something that should be easy, given the age of unlimited information in which we live, but in fact, it may be more difficult today than it was in the time of DaVinci or Franklin. By learning how to focus, we can maximize our two most valuable and limited resources (time and energy) and ensure that we're using them on the things we value most. The last thing we want is the disappointing experience of the mountain climber who spends their life climbing a great peak, only to arrive at the top and discover that they've climbed the wrong one.

---

[27] "Napping May Not Be Such a No-No," *Harvard Health Publishing*, November 1, 2009, https://www.health.harvard.edu/newsletter_article/napping-may-not-be-such-a-no-no.

This is how I got through the middle of that marathon. After the excitement at the start line was long gone and the wind and rain began taking a toll on me physically and mentally, I knew my only chance to finish was to stay focused on the goal. I reminded myself regularly of what I was trying to achieve and why I was trying to achieve it. I resisted the temptation to be distracted by the wind, rain, hills, and all the other challenging elements that come with running for four or five hours in incredibly difficult weather. And it worked. Until it didn't. More on that in a bit.

PATIENCE

The second type of resistance we encounter typically occurs between the middle and end of the process. Have you ever started a project strong, only to run out of steam and either rush to the end or just quit before you finished? I know I have.

Taking action is hard. Even when you manage to do that, then you have to find a way to stay focused and not get sidetracked along the way. Even if you manage to do both of those things, there's still the challenge of maintaining that momentum day after day, week after week, month after month, until you accomplish what you've set out to do. It's hard. It's sometimes exhausting. Many times we get to a point, usually about three-quarters of the way there, when we just run out of steam. The excitement of beginning a new project is long gone, and the anticipation of finishing is still so far off in the distance that we can't see it yet. In order to succeed, we have to find a way to keep going, even when we don't feel like it anymore.

I have run many long-distance races, five or six half-marathons, and four marathons. A marathon is 42.2 km. The fastest marathoners in the world take over two hours to complete one, but most people who run them take much, much longer. For those of us who aren't elite athletes, a marathon will typically take anywhere from three and a half to five hours to complete, and it's tough. The whole thing is challenging. In fact, I suggest that the preparation, the training required to prepare yourself to run a marathon, is even harder than actually running the race. While no part of it is easy, the toughest part has to be kilometres thirty-two through forty. That's the period I call "no-man's-land." By the time you get to kilometre nineteen or twenty, the excitement of the start line with the butter-flies in your stomach, the music, and the people cheering are all long gone. Depending on the size of the race, you find yourself running with a small group of people, or maybe even by yourself. You're also still a long way from the reward of the finish line. You just want to be done. You know that crossing that finish line will feel amazing, but it isn't coming fast enough. Logically you know it's only seven miles away, but fatigue has set in at that point. You're tired. Your legs feel heavy. You know that the next seven miles will be significantly harder to run than the first seven. You start to question whether that reward is worth the effort and the discomfort. You may even contemplate quitting.

PERSEVERANCE

Inevitably, when you make the decision to take action toward a particular goal or result you want to achieve, you'll reach that point where you just don't feel like it anymore. I've reached that point in every single long-distance race I've run, but nowhere more intensely than that first marathon.

After running for more than four hours, I had reached my break-ing point. I was starting to drag my feet. It was kilometre thirty-six, just six kilometres left until the finish line. In comparison to a for-ty-two-kilometre marathon, six kilometres is nothing. On a day with fresh legs, I could run six kilometres in a little more than half an hour. But I didn't have fresh legs. I was thoroughly exhausted. I'd been running for four hours, I was soaking wet from the rain and freezing cold from the wind, and my legs felt like lead. Those six kilometres might as well have been sixty at that point. I was running on Barrington Street in Halifax where there's a long straightaway for about a mile. I remember looking in front of me and then behind me. There was no one for as far as I could see in either direction. I was alone.

Perfect, I thought to myself, *no witnesses. I'll just sit down on the curb here and wait for someone to come pick me up.* Event organisers for endurance events are always careful to ensure that everyone who starts the race gets back safely. I knew eventually someone would come looking for me.

I was just about to sit down. Thank God I didn't, because if I had I'm quite sure I wouldn't have had the leg strength to stand back up again. Right before I sat, I looked at my hand. Before the race started, I had written on my hand some of the reasons I was running this race in the first place. Remember how we talked before about the importance of having a clear and compelling vision? I had one, and I had clearly articulated why I was running this race. Sure, I wanted the sense of accomplishment and to prove to myself and everyone else that I could do anything I set my mind to, but there was something else too. On my hand, I had written the names of three friends. Three people I had met and become close to while we were all waiting for our transplants together. Three people whose stories did not end as nicely as mine did. Each of those three people died while still on the waiting list. They were just like me, but I got lucky when a donor was found in time. As I read those names, the pain and discomfort I was feeling didn't seem quite so serious. At least I was still breathing. At least I was here. I knew then that I had to find a way to get to the finish line—or die trying.

The idea of it, though, was overwhelming. I wasn't sure I could get my legs to go another block, let alone another six kilometres, but I knew I had to try. I decided I'd start by just trying to take a step. Could I get myself moving again? I don't care how exhausted or discouraged you are, every one of us can do that.

I took one step.

Great, I thought, *now you have to do that again.* Again, I took one step.

Then another.

Then another.

For a kilometre or two, I focused only on taking one step at a time. As I gained confidence with that and started to feel a little better, I challenged myself to run from one light post to the next. Then I stretched the goal to run to the next kilometre marker, and so on, and so forth.

It took me nearly an hour to complete those last six kilometres. There was no running and very little jogging. Mostly I walked, one small step in front of the other, but I finished. After five hours and sixteen minutes in the pouring rain and blustering wind, I finished the Bluenose International Marathon. I was officially "a marathoner."

That day, I learned both the power and simplicity of perseverance. When I reached a point where the pain of continuing loomed larger than the reward of achieving the goal, the temptation was to quit. While I could never imagine it before the race began, the idea of resting on the side of the road was more appealing than continuing to move, even though I knew that was the only way to get to the finish line. That's when I needed perseverance. I couldn't allow myself to succumb to the discomfort I felt in that moment, and I couldn't be intimidated by how far I still had to go. I simply had to focus on taking one more step. When I broke down the goal to such a small and simple thing, it became manageable. I still wasn't sure I could finish, but I knew I could take another step.

I didn't know it at the time, but what I did that day was employ a tool that I have now formalised into The OMS Mindset Rule™.

THE OMS MINDSET RULE™

The O.M.S. in the OMS Mindset Rule stands for *One. More. Step.* The tool is simple but powerful. To use it, you have to make the conscious decision that you will continue to take one more step until you realize your goal. You commit to yourself that you will do whatever it takes for as long as it takes. Then, you take some kind of action, however small. Don't be intimidated by how far you have to go or how hard you know it might be. Just take the next step. I often remind people that small, consistent actions over time will always create results. The reason most people fail to achieve their goals isn't because they lack the ability; it's because they allow fear, distraction, or discouragement to stop them from taking small, consistent action over and over and over again until they get where they want to go. Don't let that be you.

This may feel like the end of the journey. If you've taken action and achieved the goal, what's left to do? The challenge that remains is to ensure that we are pursuing the right goals.

How many times have you heard someone talk about reaching a particular milestone and feeling disappointed or even empty? They worked really hard to achieve a goal only to discover that the thing they were chasing wasn't all it was cracked up to be. There are countless examples:

- The CEO who reaches the top of the corporate ladder only to feel like their life feels like a prison.
- The teacher who dreamt of moulding young minds but finds herself spending most of her time dealing with paperwork and bureaucracy.
- The nurse who longs to invest quality time with her patients but is so overworked that her patient interactions are a blur by the end of every shift.

The only thing worse than failing, is investing our precious time and energy to achieve something that doesn't matter. As we climb the ladder of success, we have to take time to ensure that the ladder isn't leaning against the wrong wall.

In the next chapter we will talk about *assessment*. This is where we evaluate what is working and what isn't. It is also where we ensure that we are still heading in the direction we want to go.

 RESILIENCE REMINDERS

- Small and consistent action over time will create results. Most people fail to realize their goals simply because they lack the consistency of continued effort and the patience to see the results.
- Being focused is challenging with so many distractions available to us each day. However, the more focussed you can be, the greater impact your efforts will have.
- Use the OMS Mindset Rule. We all have times when we question our ability to keep going. When you struggle just focus on simply taking one more step in the right direction.

ASSESSMENT

*"Be honest about how you approach failure. Don't just be
critical of yourself, because that can be self-serving.
Approach it honestly, assess your performance, and assess
the areas where you have fallen short. Correct them and
move on. Don't dwell on it. Don't hold on to it."*

—Megan Rapinoe

I grew up in and out of hospitals. Much of my first two years of life were spent in hospitals for surgeries and the recovery that came after. Then there were regular tests, check-ups, and intermittent illnesses to deal with as well. One thing I picked up from observing healthcare professionals at work is the emphasis they place on regular assessment. Nothing happens with a patient until that patient is thoroughly assessed.

Emergency rooms are particularly fascinating. No one who goes there wants to be there, and they often get a bad rap because we associate them with injury, illness, and waiting longer than we'd like to for treatment. Examining the many factors that contribute to those long waits could be the subject of another book, but if you've ever been in an emergency room you know that patients don't necessarily receive treatment in the order in which they arrive.

Firstly, in any hospital I've ever been in, patients who arrive by ambulance skip the line. They go straight to acute care or, in a real crisis, the operating room. Everyone else who walks in the door is first seen by a healthcare professional (usually a nurse) who does what they call "triage." Triage is meant to evaluate patients and sort them by the level of urgency of their cases. It sounds simple enough, but it's actually quite complex. The triage nurse must quickly and efficiently see each patient, evaluate their symptoms, decide how urgent their situation is in relation to everyone else currently being treated, and then chart a course of action. While it can be frustrating as a patient to be evaluated and then sent back to the waiting room, sometimes for hours, you can be sure when that happens it's because the triage process deemed your situation was less urgent than that of another patient.

In the world of medicine, assessment is critical at every step in the process. As a patient, you're first assessed during an initial visit when a medical professional gets a metaphorical lay of the land. What's happening? How urgent is the situation? Is there one major issue to deal with, or is it a complex mix of several? But it doesn't stop there. Once a course of treatment starts, the assessment continues to evaluate whether that treatment is working. If it is, it continues. If not, another course of treatment may be tried instead.

All of this makes perfect sense, right? If you're sick, this is exactly what you want your doctor to do. You want them to carefully assess what's going on, and then once treatment begins you want them to continue to monitor whether it's working. It's easy to recognize why assessment matters so much in this context, but I've found that we neglect its importance in other aspects of our lives.

This is why the final guidepost in the Resilience Roadmap Framework is assessment. This step is easy to omit and so we often skip it entirely. I suspect it has to do with the fact that by the time we get to this stage, we've done so much work and gained some momentum. It's tempting to think we've done enough or that the results we want will take care of themselves. The reality, however, is that this is exactly when it's critical to keep our eyes on the road. We've worked hard to get moving, and now we have momentum, but if we don't pay close attention, our speed can carry us right off the road! Momentum is fantastic. We all love to go faster toward our goals. Once we have momentum, we not only go faster but go faster with less effort. So what happens if we build speed and momentum but are going in the wrong direction? What happens if our ladder is leaning against the wrong wall? We're just getting further from our goals at a faster pace. Assessment helps us avoid that.

I have a horrible sense of direction. I use maps and GPS units all the time, sometimes even in my hometown. I've learned the hard way, more than once, what happens when we don't periodically stop to assess whether the road we're on is taking us where we want to go. Recently I was driving to pick up my daughter and her friends who had spent the day at the beach. We are fortunate to live less than twenty minutes from beautiful beaches on the eastern coast of Canada and the Atlantic Ocean, so a day trip to the beach is easy to do. I let my daughter know she could expect me in about twenty minutes. Even though I've gone to this beach dozens of times, there was construction, I wasn't paying close attention to where I was going, and I missed the turn. The problem was, it took me a long time to realize my mistake. Eventually, I passed a sign indicating that I was approaching a town totally in the wrong direction. It was then that I realized I had missed my turn and been driving the wrong way for more than fifteen minutes. It would take me twice as long to get to my daughter and her friends than I had planned.

My failure to actively assess where I was and verify that the road I was on was taking me where I wanted to go cost me about an hour that day. That's not a big deal in the grand scheme of things, but it was a powerful reminder of why it's so important to take time to assess whether the direction we've chosen and the actions we're taking are bringing us where we want to go. Practising periodic assessment will help you see things you may otherwise miss and catch issues while they're small and manageable before they become unmanageable and overwhelming. How often have you found yourself in a situation when you knew if you had just noticed there was an issue sooner, it would've been so much easier to deal with?

I used to wonder how a person could get to the point of bankruptcy before realizing they were overspending, or how someone could reach the point of clinical obesity before admitting they were eating too much. It was only after I found myself sitting in my doctor's office in a health crisis that I began to understand. Despite having taken good care of myself for most of my life, and despite knowing what symptoms to watch for, I had allowed myself to get into a medical mess. It's incredibly easy to become complacent, which is exactly why we have to periodically invest time and effort to assess whether our actions are working so that we can catch small issues before they become a crisis.

It would be nice if every decision we made was right, but that isn't a realistic expectation. The reality is that we *will* make wrong decisions. We will choose the wrong path sometimes. Or, because circumstances change regularly, what was the right path may become the wrong one later. As long as we make the time and effort to periodically assess what's working and what's not, and whether the road we're on is still the right one, we'll be fine.

Whenever we face any change or adversity, it's important to be able to effectively analyse the situation in an objective and critical fashion. We must first see the realities of the situation accurately. This step cannot be overlooked or bypassed. We often don't see things objectively, especially in the middle of a difficult situation. When we're emotionally involved in something, it's nearly impossible to be objective, yet objectivity and effective analysis is exactly what we need to make good decisions.

Regular objective assessment is a tool employed in a wide variety of settings, not only to ensure success but to identify potential issues before they grow into significant problems. For instance, I don't know any students who enjoy writing tests or exams. They fail to understand, though, that these are more than just ways to measure recall or aptitude in a particular subject. Teachers use tests, exams, and other evaluation tools as means to assess how well students are grasping what they've been taught. Without periodic assessments, there's no way to know what students have retained and what they've missed or who needs more help and who's ready to move on.

In healthcare, assessment is a similarly invaluable tool. Medical professionals use assessments such as colonoscopies and mammograms to identify disease in early stages when it's easier to treat. When a medical situation is more critical, such as when a patient is in the ICU, monitoring of vital signs and other assessments are sometimes performed several times an hour to ensure that professionals can react as quickly as possible if the current course of treatment is proving ineffective.

Like many things in our lives, however, just because we understand the value of assessment at an intellectual level doesn't mean we'll apply it. How often do we fail to pause and take stock of whether our current course of action is working? Have you ever been shocked by the balance on your credit card statement or the number staring back at you on the bathroom scale? I know I have. But if we're doing a good job of regularly assessing our financial situation and our weight, that shouldn't happen. If you check your bank balance once a month or, better yet, once a week, you'll catch your overspending before it gets to the level of raising your blood pressure. Speaking of which, if you weigh yourself once a week, you're more likely to catch a slow upward trend and be able to make the necessary adjustments to your diet or exercise habits.

In the early days of my business, I sat down with my accountant and had a rude awakening. They asked me for several key numbers about my business. Numbers that should be easy to generate and that I should've known. Numbers such as my gross revenue, my monthly expenses, and my net profit. I couldn't provide any of those. I not only didn't know the numbers off the top of my head but couldn't even calculate them from the mess I called my "accounting system." When I finally dug through my papers and did the calculations, I came to a horrifying conclusion: my business was spending more money than it was making. Not only that, but I didn't even really have a "business" in the truest sense of the word. A business pays its employees and expenses and then, hopefully, has a profit left over. At that time, I wasn't paying myself anything consistently. Whatever the business had left after expenses was my "salary," but the business made nothing. In fact, often after I had taken enough out to pay my personal bills, my business was in the red.

For years as my business "grew," I was tracking only one number: gross revenue. That number was getting bigger, so I thought of myself as quite successful. What I failed to consider was that as my business grew, so did the expenses to run it. I was also paying myself a little better each year, so when it came to net revenue, there was none. My perception of my business when someone would ask me was that it was going very well. I was making $60,000–$75,000 a year in sales. As a twenty-something kid running his first business, I felt pretty good about that. I was a success story, I thought. But when my accountant and I looked at what my real net revenue was after expenses and paying myself something, the reality was glaringly different.

It takes courage and strength to face the hard truths of our lives. It was very difficult for me to look at the realities of my business and admit that it wasn't working as well as I thought it was. Part of me was resistant and wanted to justify what I'd done and how I'd done it, trying to find a good excuse for what I was seeing in the numbers. *There must be a mistake. Maybe the math was wrong, or maybe my line of business is just different.* Eventually, however, I had to humble myself and admit that numbers don't lie. I wasn't an exception. I was like every small business: if I wasn't making a profit, I wasn't making any money.

After completing that assessment, I was then able to use the Resilience Roadmap Framework from the beginning to rebuild a solid foundation for my business. I acknowledged the problems identified during the assessment and accepted that I wasn't an accountant or financial planner. Managing my business's finances alone was not a plan for success, so I sought help from my accountant. Together we crafted a new aspiration for my finances and made the necessary adaptations to the way I was doing things. Finally, we put together a plan of action to help me achieve my new goals. Today my business is on very solid footing. In fact, thanks to the new plan we put in place, I was able to take my wife on an all-expenses paid trip to Hawaii using the profits from my business. Profits that wouldn't have existed if we hadn't made the effort to do an honest assessment of how things were working (or weren't).

To be great at making the right adjustment at the right time, you have to be willing to accept the possibility that your current course of action may not be right. You must be open to the possibility that you're wrong, or at least that you're no longer right. To find out how well your current course of action is working or if you need to adjust and change direction, use a tool I call The Action Assessment Checklist™.

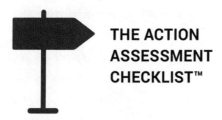

THE ACTION ASSESSMENT CHECKLIST™

Here are five essential questions to ask yourself when evaluating your current course of action:

1. **What's working?**

   When you look at your situation, what's working well? Sometimes adjustment means making just a minor tweak. If most things are going the way you want them to, chances are good that you don't need to completely overhaul your plan. All that may be required is for you to adjust a few things.

   Starbucks, for example, was on the right track from the beginning. Coffee was their key ingredient. High-quality coffee beans are as much a part of their success today as they were in the very beginning of their story. What Howard Shultz did after his trip to Italy wasn't completely overhauling how the company did business, but simply adding a new piece to the business that helped its sales numbers leap.

2. **What's not working?**

It's important to be clear about exactly what isn't working in our lives. Sometimes we get a sense that something "just isn't right," but we aren't sure what it is. We may make the mistake of trying random changes in the hope of discovering what's wrong. While that approach may work some of the time, taking the time at the front end to carefully examine what's going on so we can isolate the problem is much more effective.

For example, you may find that your energy level is far too low. This may lead you down the path of investigating thyroid issues, stress management, and a host of other possible causes. Later you may discover the real issue was that you were chronically dehydrated (most of us are), and simply by adding a few litres of water to your daily diet you notice major improvements to how you feel. Do some investigation and be sure to start with the most obvious causes. We're often tempted to assume the cause is more complicated than it is.

3. **How have I changed?**

You can ask yourself many questions to help figure out whether something is going on with you that's causing you to feel the way you feel. For example, has something happened in your life recently that's causing you to think, feel, or act differently than normal? Have you started eating differently? Are you exercising more or less than usual? Are you getting enough sleep? Are you particularly stressed out at work?

Because you're with yourself every day, it's easy for changes that take place slowly over time to go unnoticed. When I got really sick before my transplant, I lost a third of my body weight in three months, but since the pounds came off a tiny bit at a time and I wasn't paying attention, I didn't notice. Changes can be physical, mental, and emotional. To help spot them, it can be helpful to do a periodic check-in with yourself to see how you've changed.

4. **How have others changed?**

Look at how your external environment, including the people you spend time with, has changed. Typically when things are feeling off in our lives, we assume it's something we've done. While that can be the case, the changes are often external. Maybe your friend who's been treating you differently lately is going through something difficult, and their behaviour has nothing to do with you and everything to do with how they're feeling. Maybe your boss is having marriage troubles, and the fact that they came down hard on you yesterday has nothing to do with your performance and everything to do with your boss's mood.

5. **Where do we go from here?**

All the investigation and introspection above is little more than navel-gazing unless we use it to take action. The whole point of going through this part of the Resilience Roadmap is to see what has happened and possibly make constructive adjustments. If you have new information but continue to make the same decisions, you haven't adjusted anything. As the saying goes, "Doing the same thing and expecting different results is the definition of insanity."

In a challenging situation there are typically several possible courses of action. We often become paralyzed during the process of trying to decide which option is best. Choosing to do nothing, however, is still making a choice. So if you're going to make a decision, let it be one that's constructive. Choose the best course of action given the information you have, understanding that if it doesn't work out for some reason you can always go back and try something else. Failure isn't fatal.

Assessment is a part of success. Learning how to be comfortable with the necessity for course correcting is an important skill that every resilient person must master. The better you get at being able to adjust without taking the failure personally, the more effective you'll be at effectively facing the adversities of life.

 RESILIENCE REMINDERS

- Assessment allows us to diagnose small issues before they become major issues.
- Use assessment to delineate the things you are doing that are working from those that are no longer serving you.
- Don't be afraid to change direction if you discover that your plan of action is now taking you away from your ultimate goal.

THE BIGGEST MISTAKE

*"You can't achieve anything entirely by yourself.
There's a support system that is a basic requirement
of human existence. To be happy and successful on earth,
you just have to have people that you rely on."*

—Michael Schur

Helen Keller's story has always amazed, inspired, and mystified me. Helen Adams Keller was born in Tuscumbia, Alabama, on June 27, 1860. When Keller was nineteen months old, she contracted an illness that doctors described as "an acute congestion of the stomach and the brain."[28] People now believe this to be scarlet fever or meningitis, which left Keller both deaf and blind.

---

[28] Google Arts & Culture, "The Inspiring Story of Helen Keller," accessed August 28, 2022, https://artsandculture.google.com/story/the-inspiring-story-of-helen-keller/tAVh-1jWXeX_KQ?hl=en.

You may be familiar with Keller's story. You're certainly familiar with the terms *blind* and *deaf.* But do we really appreciate the practical implications for someone dealing with these challenges?

Stop here for a minute. Imagine what your life would be like if you woke up tomorrow without the ability to see or hear. I've sometimes had debates with friends about which would be harder to cope with, being blind or being deaf. It's hard to know for sure without experiencing it, but for me, I think blindness would be more difficult to cope with. Not being able to see my wife's or children's faces, never seeing a sunset again, not being able to drive, and the loss of independence that would involve are very scary thoughts. I'm sure it's difficult to be deaf as well. Which do you think would be hardest for you?

Now imagine that overnight you lost the ability to see and hear. Consider how disorienting and scary that would be. Consider how helpless you'd feel. How frustrating would it be to become completely dependent on someone else to do anything? Maybe after a few minutes of seriously considering this, we can get the tiniest appreciation for what the life of Helen Keller must've been like.

We also have to remember that Helen Keller grew up in rural Alabama in the late 1880s, when modern medical facilities and the technology, testing, and support networks we have today didn't exist. The American Foundation for the Blind, an organization for which Keller would work for more than forty years, wasn't founded until 1921. Imagine how isolated and alone she and her family must've felt. In 1862, the natural response to the situation the Kellers found themselves in when Helen awoke from her illness blind and deaf would be despair. After all, in rural Alabama with little to no resources and no background in working with, educating, or raising a child with her level of disability, what were they supposed to do?

Imagine yourself in a similar situation. Imagine being the parents of that young child in that environment. Imagine how all the hopes and dreams you have for that child would change. What's the best you could expect for her life? I think it's fair to say that neither of her parents would have imagined in her early childhood days what Keller would eventually accomplish.

She was educated at the Perkins school for the blind where she learned how to read, write, and eventually speak. By putting her fingers on the lips of her teacher, Keller learned how to "read" lips and speak. This fact alone is remarkable, but it was only the beginning. Keller went on from the Perkins school to study at Radcliffe College, where she became the first deaf and blind person ever to graduate with a Bachelor of Arts degree. After Radcliffe, Keller dedicated her life to improving the lives of others who suffered from similar disabilities. She travelled the world visiting more than twenty countries, lecturing, writing, and raising money. By the end of her life, she had written and published more than a dozen books and articles. She helped found the American Civil Liberties Union and also enjoyed acting, performing in two films. For her great humanitarian work, Keller was recognized with several awards including an honorary doctorate from Harvard University, the Presidential Medal of Freedom, Brazil's Order of the Southern Cross, the Philippines' Golden Heart, and Japan's Sacred Treasure, and she was named one of the twentieth century's Most Important People of the Century by *Life Magazine*.

By any standard, Helen Keller was one of the most prolific people ever to walk the face of the earth, and she did it all while being unable to see or hear. To say that she was resilient in the face of adversity would be a gross understatement. There's a reason, however, that I've saved Keller's example for this part of the book. I think it's fair to say that Helen Keller would be the first to admit she could never have done any of what she did alone.

Our society is one that values fierce independence and individuality. We love the idea of the hero who pulls themselves up by their bootstraps, pushes everyone aside, and sets out to prove they can accomplish whatever they set their mind to. Particularly when it comes to stories of heroic resilience, it's tempting to think in only individualistic terms. The reality, however, is far different. Without strong social connections and systemic support, even those with the most resilient character who are following the most proven resilience models are unlikely to succeed. Quite simply, we can't climb the mountain of adversity on our own. In order to succeed, we need a network of people and systems to support our efforts.

Common sense supports this idea. What do we do with our children when they misbehave? We send them to their room to be alone. As they get older, we may "ground" them, taking away their ability to socialize with their friends. As adults, if we break the rules of our society, we're separated from society and locked up in prison. As a prisoner, if we break the rules, we're sent to solitary confinement. We are social creatures by nature, and we need the support of each other to live and to thrive. When this is taken away, it only makes sense that we're unable to be our best.

Psychologists looking at this phenomenon in a number of situations have concluded the same thing: those who are surrounded by supportive people and live in places with a network of support— including things such as good schools, quality hospitals, and close-knit communities—fare better than others. The term psychologists use for these social support structures is "resource factors." When we speak about dysfunction or disease, we use the term "risk factors." For example, if you have high blood pressure and are overweight, you have two of the major risk factors for developing heart disease. That doesn't mean you absolutely will develop it, but your chances are much higher than someone without those risk factors. Resource factors work the same way but in reverse. Someone who has positive self-esteem, possesses a problem-solving approach to life, and comes from a supporting two-parent home has three of the resource factors for greater resilience. That doesn't mean that person will absolutely be able to bounce back from anything they may face, but their chances are much better than someone who doesn't possess those same resource factors.

Resource factors can be internal or external. There are resource factors that exist within an individual and those that exist in the home, community, or society. For example, internal resource factors include a high sense of self-efficacy and self-worth. A person who possesses these internal resource factors will do better than someone who doesn't. External resource factors include close friendships and strong communities. Someone who lives in these environments will do better than someone who doesn't. Of course, these two sets of factors work together and affect each other, which is more important depending on the individual. In fact, there's a third set of factors called "differential susceptibility."[29] Differential susceptibility explains why a resource factor may be helpful for one person and not another or why a risk factor may have a great impact on one person and not another. Research indicates that the strongest and most critical external resource factor is likely the strength of our relationships with those closest to us: our family and friends. This would explain why someone who lives in a wealthy country like the United States may still find themselves on the street and unable to overcome their challenges. The social support structures and resources are available (though perhaps not as easily accessible as we'd like them to be), but that alone isn't enough to overcome a lack of familial connection and support.

---

[29] Bruce J. Ellis et al., "Differential Susceptibility to the Environment: An Evolutionary—Neurodevelopmental Theory," *Development and Psychopathology* 23, no. 1 (February 2011): 7–28, https://doi.org/10.1017/S0954579410000611.

To survive and certainly to thrive, we all need other people in our lives. As social beings, we can only be our best when we're living in and connected to a society with strong social bonds. Resilient people are almost always those with strong connections to friends and family, a resilience factor that can be easily overlooked. Despite our fierce sense of independence and individuality in Western culture, our need for each other is undeniable. If you want to be more resilient, focus on strengthening your social bonds.

When Hellen Keller was six years old, she met Anne Sullivan. At that time, Keller had virtually no way to communicate other than some basic expressions of desire such as pulling her parents in the direction she wanted to go. In 1887, Sullivan began working with Keller as her teacher and governess. Sullivan taught Keller how by signing into each other's hands they could communicate with each other. Keller, however, noticed that Sullivan, who had learned to speak, did not use signs when she communicated with others. Sullivan helped Keller understand that people could speak to each other using their mouths. Seeing her curiosity, Sullivan put Keller's hands on her mouth and throat as she spoke so that Helen could "feel" her speech. Instantly Keller signed, "I want to learn how to talk with my mouth."

It took a great deal of experimentation and patience, but eventually the two discovered a system that worked. By putting Helen's hand in a position such that her first finger rested on Sullivan's lips, the second finger on the nose, and her thumb on her throat, Keller could feel the vibration of the spoken word. After seven lessons, Keller was able to say, "I am not dumb now."[30]

---

[30] TransformingArt, "(Rare!) Helen Keller & Anne Sullivan (1930 Newsreel Footage)," YouTube, June 27, 2009, video, 2:58, https://www.youtube.com/watch?v=GvluLfF35Uw.

Sullivan's support of Keller extended far beyond teacher–student. The two became lifelong companions, living together for the remainder of Sullivan's life. It's undeniably her support and Keller's persistence that allowed Keller to accomplish all that she did.

As I've written about already in this book, I've lived a life dealing with chronic illness. From birth to age twenty-five, I was in and out of hospitals often and dealt with a variety of health challenges, culminating in a heart and double-lung transplant in 2002 when I had a six-month hospital stay. During my time spent in hospitals, I witnessed the impact that family and friends had on a patient's resilience. I feel incredibly blessed that I had two selfless and dedicated parents who made me and my health their number one priority. When I was an infant, they were both at my bedside whenever possible. Throughout my teen and young-adult years, they would travel with me to all my doctors' appointments. They let me speak and ask questions of the doctor, but they were also there taking notes, asking questions, and ensuring that I understood what the doctor was saying and what I had to do. More importantly, they provided much-needed emotional support.

When I was finally listed for my transplant in the fall of 2001, I had to move to Toronto, over a thousand miles from home, to be near the transplant centre that performed the rare surgery. The staff of the transplant program there informed us that I could only be accepted on the transplant list there if I had an "accompanying person" with me at all times. The support person could be a parent, partner, child, or friend, but every patient needed to have someone there. I was also encouraged to attend regular support group meetings.

As a twenty-three-year-old man who considered himself autonomous and strong, this requirement was silly. *I don't need anyone with me*, I thought. After all, I'd been living on my own for a few years, was looking forward to moving to the "big city," and even had a few friends and family members in Toronto. So if I ever really needed anything, they were just a phone call away. I certainly didn't need my mommy and daddy to come with me. I was a grown man for goodness' sake. But I was told in no uncertain terms that I didn't have a choice.

When we met with the transplant team the first time, the social worker explained to me that I was invited to attend the weekly support group meeting for all those who were waiting for a lung transplant. I didn't want to go, but I was told that I had to go at least once. Begrudgingly, Dad and I showed up to a small room in the hospital a few days later.

As soon as I walked into the room, I knew I didn't want to stay. There were about a dozen or so patients and their "support person" sitting in a circle. Most of them had oxygen masks and tanks because they were suffering from end-stage lung diseases. I was the only person waiting for a heart AND lung transplant instead of just lungs, and my disease was caused by my heart. So while my heart and lungs weren't working properly, my breathing was quite good, and I was the only patient in the room not on oxygen. I looked around the room and immediately noticed something else that separated me from nearly everyone else: I was thirty years younger than almost everyone in the room. *Great,* I thought, *I'm going to have to sit here and listen to a bunch of old people complain about their problems.* I relented to stay for the rest of that meeting but had no plans to return ever again.

The first few meetings went almost as I predicted. The leaders of the group, Bruce and Linda, who had received their transplants already, led the group in discussions about various aspects of transplant, the varying diseases everyone was suffering with, and the things we could do to try to cope with the waiting. If I had been open-minded, I could've admitted that some of the information was quite helpful, but I was young and stubborn and didn't believe I needed this group or these people, let alone the information they had to share. But since I wasn't working and we were usually at the hospital that day of the week for tests anyway, I didn't have much of a reason not to go.

As the weeks turned into months, I began to feel more comfortable with the people in the room. I began to form friendships. We shared a common experience, and when that experience is facing death, bonds are formed quickly. I began to trust and care about the people there. As time passed, some would get "the call." There was always a lot of joy and excitement in the room on those days, as well as tangible but unspoken tension. We'd be concerned and hopeful for the person in surgery, but we'd also wonder when it would be our turn. I often felt guilty about feeling that way. Talking to others who were waiting and knowing they felt the same way helped me cope.

At the beginning of the process, Mom and Dad made a commitment that one of them would be with me at all times. Every few months they'd switch places with each other, one moving back home to care for my three brothers and work to pay the bills, the other moving up to Toronto with me. I waited on the transplant list for nearly a year before a suitable donor was found for me. I was in the hospital as a full-time resident for the last six months of that wait. The only things that kept me sane and in relatively good spirits were my parents and friends who visited faithfully every day, and that support group.

We all need each other. We need connections. We need support. Even the strongest and most independent person you know needs at least one other person they can rely on. You can't be resilient without it.

Look at your life right now. Make a list of the people you consider your strongest connections. Who can you really count on, no matter what, when things get tough? Who can you call at 2:00 a.m. just because you need someone to talk to? Most of us have a lot of acquaintances but not nearly as many friends. We may have 1500 friends according to Facebook, but the real friends are the ones you can count on when things are toughest. Who are those people for you?

CONCLUSION

Resilience is the most critical skill of the twenty-first century. In an age of continuous and dramatic change, the only solution is to be prepared for whatever may come next. We aren't very good at predicting the specifics of the changes we will face, so it's tempting to try to anticipate every possible scenario and eventuality and develop the solutions to solve them all. While that approach may be warranted in specific instances, we'll quickly exhaust ourselves if we attempt to do it all the time. The sheer number of potential issues is too large and varied. Rather than preparing every possible solution to every possible problem, we must instead focus on building our capacity to handle whatever may come our way.

As individual citizens, we have virtually no control over many of the significant forces that impact our lives. Matters like the economy, the environment, and government are things we can have a say in, but they are certainly not things we can control. So what are we to do?

If you can't stop it from raining, make sure you take the time to buy an umbrella. That's what building resilience is all about. We know it will rain. That's life. Bad things will happen. There will be job loss and career change, relationship conflict and financial struggle, illness and death. These things are not in question; they are an inevitable part of life. The question is not "Will they happen?" but rather "WHEN will they happen?"

Life is full of challenges, obstacles, and trials. Life is also a beautiful and wonderful gift. It's a fantastic thing. We are better able to appreciate that fact when we're equipped to cope with the inevitable challenges and take them in stride and when we aren't surprised when things are difficult because we know that's how it's supposed to be.

This book has given you the tools you need to handle everything that may ever come your way. I don't know what you've faced already nor what you'll face in the future, but I do know this: If you've read this book and applied what you've read, then you're ready. You can confidently stand tall and declare that whatever happens, you will not only survive, but thrive.

ACKNOWLEDGEMENTS

Writing a book is one the hardest things I've ever done—and I have done some hard things. I started this book years ago and then life got busy. It sat on a shelf, half-written, for three years before I finally picked it back up, dusted it off, and committed to finishing it. The journey from the first words to the finished product was only completed thanks to the prodding and support of many people.

First to my wife and partner Marise. Since the early days of our marriage when you encouraged me to leave a steady income to launch my speaking business full-time, you have been my rock and the CEO of our family. I could not do what I do without you doing what you do so well. Despite the extra burden it puts on you, you have always been my greatest cheerleader. Thank you for letting me live my dream.

To our three children, Emma, Matteo, and Caleb, I love you more than I thought was humanly possible before you were born. I believe in you. I hope I can be the father you deserve.

They say you can pick your friends, but you can't pick your family. Even if I'd been able to pick, I couldn't have done better. To mom and dad, this was a book about resilience and how I believe anyone is capable of becoming resilient, but it is infinitely easier when you win the parent lottery. It has taken becoming a parent myself to really appreciate the many gifts you gave me as a child. I wouldn't be the man I am today without your wisdom, strength, patience, and guidance.

To my brothers, Neil, Greg, and Scott. You are all in this book in some way because you helped shape the person I am today. You also made tremendous personal sacrifices at a critical time in your life, to allow me to have mom and dad's support through the hardest year of my life. I will always be grateful to you for that.

To my colleagues, friends, and especially my fellow mastermind members: Azadeh, Beverly, Joel, Merge, Paul, Tyler, and Scott. Your encouragement, guidance, and feedback helped me shape a collection of concepts into a keynote presentation that has now reached thousands, and this book which will hopefully help many more. Thank you. Your excellence inspires me to continually up my game.

A book like this requires a team. To my publisher Publish Your Purpose, thank you for believing in this book and believing in me. Even when I contracted covid and fell behind schedule, you were there to get me moving again and ensure that this book got done. Bailly, my book sherpa. I know your title is "project manager" but you have been much more than that. Without your guidance and advice, this book may never have been finished and it certainly would be as good as it is. Nancy, my amazing editor. You took a decent book and turned it into something much better. Thank you for your guidance and patience. Cornelia, my cover designer. You developed so many iterations of this cover that I fully expected you to throw up your hands. Thank you for striking with me until we found the perfect fit.

To the mentors and partners who have helped me become a better speaker, coach, and author. Martin Latulippe, Dan Martell, and Stu Saunders, you have always been there to answer my questions, give me advice, and support my efforts even though there was nothing in it for you. I hope I can one day pay forward all that you have given me.

Al Phillips and Kim King. You were the first speakers bureaus who gave me a shot when I was starting out in this business. For a long time, you were the only two. Thank you for believing that a twenty-sixyear-old kid from Moncton, NB could make it in this business.

To the more than seven hundred clients who have entrusted me to speak at your events. I am eternally grateful to you. It is no small thing when someone invests valuable resources so that you can share your content with their people. I never take it for granted.

Finally, to you reading this book. Thank you for investing the money to buy this book and the time to read it. It is my life's mission to help as many people as I can realize their capacity to be resilient. I hope the ideas in this book positively impact your life as they have for thousands who have heard them already.

BIBLIOGRAPHY

Bureau of Labor Statistics. "Employment Characteristics of
    Families—2021." U.S. Department of Labor, April 20, 2022.
    https://www.bls.gov/news.release/pdf/famee.pdf.

Carey, Benedict. "Denial Makes the World Go Round."
    New York Times, November 20, 2007. https://www.nytimes.
    com/2007/11/20/health/20iht-20deni.8402176.html.

De Bruin, Tabitha. "Terry Fox." The Canadian Encyclopedia,
    last modified August 5, 2020. https://www.thecanadian
    encyclopedia.ca/en/article/terry-fox.

Ellis, Bruce J., W. Thomas Boyce, Jay Belsky, Marian J.
    Bakermans-Kranenburg, and Marinus H. van Ijzendoorn.
    "Differential Susceptibility to the Environment:
    An Evolutionary–Neurodevelopmental Theory."
    Development and Psychopathology 23, no. 1 (February 2011):
    7–28. https://doi.org/10.1017/S0954579410000611.

Forleo, Marie. *Everything is Figureoutable.* New York: Portfolio/Penguin, 2019.

Frankl, Viktor E. *Man's Search for Meaning.* Boston: Beacon Press, 2006.

Google Arts & Culture. "The Inspiring Story of Helen Keller." Accessed August 28, 2022. https://artsandculture. google.com/story/the-inspiring-story-of-helen-keller/ tAVh-1jWXeX_KQ?hl=en.

Harvard Health Publishing. "Napping May Not Be Such a No-No." November 1, 2009. https://www.health.harvard.edu/ newsletter_article/napping-may-not-be-such-a-no-no.

Heriot, Drew, dir. *The Secret.* 2006; Melbourne: Prime Time Productions, 2006. DVD.

Hendry, Erica R. "7 Epic Fails Brought to You by the Genius Mind of Thomas Edison." *Smithsonian Magazine*, November 20, 2013. https://www.smithsonianmag.com/innovation/ 7-epic-fails-brought-to-you-by-the-genius-mind-of-thomas-edison-180947786/.

Hug, James J. "Frustration Effects after Varied Numbers of Partial and Continuous Reinforcements: Incentive Differences as a Function of Reinforcement Percentage." *Psychonomic Science* 21 (1970): 57–59. https://doi.org/10.3758/BF03332433.

Huth, Susanna. "Employees Waste 759 Hours Each Year Due to Workplace Distractions." *The Telegraph*, June 22, 2015. https://www.telegraph.co.uk/finance/jobs/11691728/Employees-waste-759-hours-each-year-due-to-workplace-distractions.html.

King Jr., Martin Luther. "I Have a Dream." Lincoln Memorial, Washington DC, Transcript, The Avalon Project, Yale Law School: Lillian Goldman Law Library, August 28, 1963. https://avalon.law.yale.edu/20th_century/mlk01.asp.

Life Insurance Marketing and Research Association.
     "Life Insurance Awareness Month (2022)." Accessed
     December 14, 2022. https://www.limra.com/en/
     newsroom/liam/.

Lunden, Ingrid. "6.1B Smartphone Users Globally By 2020,
     Overtaking Basic Fixed Phone Subscriptions." TechCrunch,
     June 2, 2015. https://techcrunch.com/2015/06/02/6-1b-
     smartphone-users-globally-by-2020-overtaking-basic-fixed-
     phone-subscriptions/.

Marcus, A. M. *The Elephant and the Rope*. Scotts Valley, CA:
     CreateSpace Independent Publishing, 2015.

Ohliger, Paul. "Acceptance Was the Answer." In *Alcoholics
     Anonymous: The Big Book*, 4th ed. New York: Alcoholics
     Anonymous World Services, Inc., 2001.

Pinkney, Jerry, and Aesop. *The Tortoise & the Hare*. New York, NY:
     Boston, Little, Brown and Company, 2013.

Robison, Jennifer. "Too Many Interruptions at Work?"
     Gallup Business Journal, June 8, 2006. https://news.gallup.com/
     businessjournal/23146/too-many-interruptions-work.aspx.

Rotter, Julian. "Generalized Expectancies for Internal versus
     External Control of Reinforcement." *Psychological Monographs*
     80, no. 1 (1966): 1–28. https://doi.org/10.1037/h0092976.

Seligman, Martin E., and Steven F. Maier. "Failure to Escape
     Traumatic Shock." *Journal of Experimental Psychology* 74, no. 1:
     1–9. https://doi.org/10.1037/h0024514.

Stothart, Cary, Ainsley Mitchum, and Courtney Yehnert.
     "The Attentional Cost of Receiving a Cell Phone Notification."
     *Journal of Experimental Psychology: Human Perception
     and Performance* 41(4): 893–897. https://doi.org/10.1037/
     xhp0000100.

Thornton, Bill, Alyson Faires, Maija Robbins, and Eric Rollins.
"The Mere Presence of a Cell Phone May Be Distracting:
Implications for Attention and Task Performance."
Social Psychology 45, no. 6 (2014): 479–488. https://doi.org/
10.1027/1864-9335/a000216.

TransformingArt. "(Rare!) Helen Keller & Anne Sullivan
(1930 Newsreel Footage)." YouTube. June 27, 2009. Video,
2:58. https://www.youtube.com/watch?v=Gv1uLfF35Uw.

Watts, Alan, and Al Chung-liang Huang. *Tao: The Watercourse
Way.* New York: Pantheon Books, 1975; original Chinese
parable written by Laozi in *The Tao Te Ching*, circa 400 BC.

Winfield, Chris. "This Is Warren Buffett's Best Investment
Advice." *Time*, July 23, 2015. https://time.com/3968806/
warren-buffett-investment-advice/.

Wing, Rena R., and Suzanne Phelan. "Long-Term Weight Loss
Maintenance." *The American Journal of Clinical Nutrition*
82, no. 1 (July 2005): 222S–225S. https://doi.org/10.1093/
ajcn/82.1.222S.

Zacks. "7 Fun Facts about Starbucks in Honor of Its IPO's 25th
Anniversary." NASDAQ. June 26, 2017. www.nasdaq.com/
articles/7-fun-facts-about-starbucks-honor-its-ipos-25th-
anniversary-2017-06-26.

Ziglar, Tom. "If You Aim at Nothing . . ." Ziglar.com. Accessed
August 23, 2022. https://www.ziglar.com/articles/if-you-
aim-at-nothing-2/.

BRING
MARK BLACK
TO YOUR NEXT EVENT

Mark is an in-demand speaker at corporate and association events all over the world. He is one of less than 1600 speakers on the globe with the Certified Speaking Professional designation.

Mark's client list includes ExxonMobil, Mercedes Benz, Million Dollar Roundtable, Scotiabank, and hundreds of others.

> *When Mark came on stage, he immediately connected with the audience. It was amazing to see how people truly listened to what he had to say. Mark Black is THE keynote speaker you need for your event.*
>
> **—Mercedes Benz**

For more information about bringing Mark to your next event, go to: markblack.ca or contact us directly: Jenn@MarkBlack.ca

TAKE THE
RESILIENCE QUOTIENT
ASSESSMENT™

How resilient are you right now? Want to find out? Take the assessment today. Then, after you read the book and implement the strategies, take the assessment again and see how far you have come.

https://markblack.ca/resiliencequotientassessment

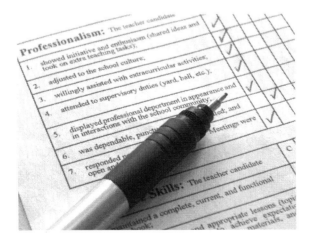

WORK WITH MARK AS YOUR COACH WITH
BREAKTHROUGH COACHING FOR INDIVIDUALS AND GROUPS

Why should you work with a coach? Isn't that just for athletes? No. In fact, every high-performer in any field has a coach. It is the shortest route to get from where you are to where you want to be.

Clarity

Most people fail to achieve their goals primarily because they lack clarity about what they want. With Mark as your coach, you will get clarity around what you want and why it matters to you, and then create the action plan to achieve it.

Accountability

Most of us are bad at keeping promises to ourselves, but we are quite good at keeping our commitments to others. When you hire a coach, you use this to your advantage. Having a coach forces you to take action.

Objectivity

We all struggle at times. No one is completely objective about their own situation. The unbiased sounding board that a coach provides, goes a long way to helping you get the perspective needed to solve your problems.

CHOOSE YOUR PACKAGE
BREAKTHROUGH COACHING
FOR INDIVIDUALS AND GROUPS

The Breakthrough Advisory™ – 1-on-1 Coaching

Get unstuck, be accountable, and finally execute all of the things you know you "should" do. One-on-one coaching may be the most powerful tool to help you grow and realize your potential.

You will make more progress in three months working one-on-one than in a year on your own. Mark's clients have increased revenue, improved relationships, and more.

The Breakthrough Blueprint™ – Post-Event Implementation

Keep the momentum flowing with ongoing support. Mark will work with your team on an ongoing basis to help them implement the strategies he shares in his keynotes and workshops.

Using regularly scheduled follow-up webinars and live Q&As, Mark will work with you to ensure that people in your organization are implementing.

The Breakthrough Huddle™ – Team Coaching

You want to get the most out of every person on your team. Whether you run a business or an association, you need all hands on deck executing at their best to achieve your objectives.

Mark will work with you to clarify values and goals and create an action plan to ensure that everyone is pulling in the same direction.

For more information, email: Mark@MarkBlack.ca

The B Corp Movement

Dear reader,

Thank you for reading this book and joining the Publish Your Purpose community! You are joining a special group of people who aim to make the world a better place.

What's Publish Your Purpose About?
Our mission is to elevate the voices often excluded from traditional publishing. We intentionally seek out authors and storytellers with diverse backgrounds, life experiences, and unique perspectives to publish books that will make an impact in the world.

Certified

Corporation

Beyond our books, we are focused on tangible, action-based change. As a woman- and LGBTQ+-owned company, we are committed to reducing inequality, lowering levels of poverty, creating a healthier environment, building stronger communities, and creating high-quality jobs with dignity and purpose.

As a Certified B Corporation, we use business as a force for good. We join a community of mission-driven companies building a more equitable, inclusive, and sustainable global economy. B Corporations must meet high standards of transparency, social and environmental performance, and accountability as determined by the nonprofit B Lab. The certification process is rigorous and ongoing (with a recertification requirement every three years).

How Do We Do This?
We intentionally partner with socially and economically disadvantaged businesses that meet our sustainability goals. We embrace and encourage our authors and employee's differences in race, age, color, disability, ethnicity, family or marital status, gender identity or expression, language, national origin, physical and mental ability, political affiliation, religion, sexual orientation, socio-economic status, veteran status, and other characteristics that make them unique.

Community is at the heart of everything we do—from our writing and publishing programs to contributing to social enterprise nonprofits like reSET (https://www.resetco.org/) and our work in founding B Local Connecticut.

We are endlessly grateful to our authors, readers, and local community for being the driving force behind the equitable and sustainable world we are building together.

To connect with us online, or publish with us,
visit us at www.publishyourpurpose.com.

Elevating Your Voice,

Jenn T Grace

Jenn T. Grace
Founder, Publish Your Purpose

Made in the USA
Columbia, SC
09 June 2024

36394532R00124